FILMMAKERS SERIES
edited by
ANTHONY SLIDE

Making Music with Charlie Chaplin

An Autobiography
by

ERIC JAMES

Filmmakers Series, No. 71

The Scarecrow Press, Inc.
Lanham, Maryland, and London
2000

SCARECROW PRESS, INC.

Published in the United States of America
by Scarecrow Press, Inc.
4720 Boston Way, Lanham, Maryland 20706
http://www.scarecrowpress.com

4 Pleydell Gardens, Folkestone
Kent CT20 2DN, England

British Library Cataloguing in Publication Information Available

Library of Congress Cataloging-in-Publication Data

James, Eric, 1913–
    Making music with Charlie Chaplin : an autobiography / by Eric James.
        p. cm. — (Filmmakers series ; no. 71)
    Includes index.
    ISBN 0-8108-3741-2 (cloth : alk. paper)
     1. James, Eric, 1913– 2. Pianists—England—Biography. 3. Chaplin,
    Charlie, 1889–1977.   I. Title. II. Series.
ML417.J33 A3 2000
786.2'092—dc21
[B]   99-054369

♾™ The paper used in this publication meets the minimum requirements of
American National Standard for Information Sciences—Permanence of
Paper for Printed Library Materials, ANSI/NISO Z39.48–1992.
Manufactured in the United States of America.

To my wife, Phyllis

Contents

Acknowledgments

With special thanks to
Dorothy Joyce, Averil Sutthery, and Joan Joyce—not forgetting
my stepdaughter Julia Hitchcock and her husband
Vodeck Fedorowicz, without whose help this book would
never have been completed.

With a special acknowledgment and grateful thanks to
Jeffrey Vance (coauthor of *Wife of the Life of the Party*),
whose advice and professional guidance were invaluable.

Introduction

$\mathcal{C}$harles Chaplin was not a classically trained musician, yet he is credited with the composition of all of his film scores. Charles Chaplin was not a composer, yet the musical accompaniment to his films indelibly bear his unique stamp. Charles Chaplin was not a songwriter, yet several of his songs are still rerecorded and enjoyed today. It is impossible to reconcile Chaplin's enigmatic and inexorable link to music without uncovering its roots and tracing its development, beginning with a simple melody wafting through Kennington Cross in turn-of-the-century London.

Charles Chaplin's conception of music began with a rather mystical encounter with a pair of street musicians at Kennington Cross. As a young, impoverished, and impressionable boy living in London a century ago, Chaplin came across two musicians playing a rendition of "The Honeysuckle and the Bee" on a clarinet and a harmonium. Chaplin later described the moment in life-altering terms:

> It was here that I first discovered music, or where I first learned its rare beauty, a beauty that has gladdened and haunted me from that moment. It all happened one night while I was there, about midnight. I recall the whole thing so distinctly.
>
> I was just a boy, and its beauty was like some sweet mystery. I did not understand. I only knew I loved it and I became reverent as the sounds carried themselves through my brain *via* my heart.

> I suddenly became aware of a harmonica [sic] and a
> clarinet playing a weird, harmonious message. I learned
> later that it was "The Honeysuckle and the Bee." It was
> played with such feeling that I became conscious for the
> first time of what melody really was. My first awakening
> to music.[1]

Chaplin described this as the exact moment that "music first
entered my soul."[2]

More than a half century later, a melancholy Chaplin evoked
this memory in *Limelight* with a simple melody played by a clarinet and harmonium that lulls Calvero to sleep before the film's
first dream sequence, the flea circus routine.

Chaplin's musical education was not confined to the streets of
London. Both of Chaplin's parents were music hall entertainers,
and Chaplin grew up absorbing the popular songs of the day.

Undoubtedly Chaplin's early connection with music was
closely tied to his comedic gifts. At the base of Chaplin's own
pantomimic performances are driving balletic rhythms, consonant
with musical composition. Chaplin's early career in the English
music halls with the Fred Karno Company was literally under-
scored by music. Each Karno pantomime utilized music as a counterpoint to comedic action. In a 1952 BBC radio interview, Chaplin
acknowledged this influence:

> They [Karno sketches] had splendid music. For instance,
> if they had squalor surroundings with a lot of comedy
> tramps working in it, then, you see, they would have very
> beautiful boudoir music, something of the eighteenth cen-
> tury, very lush and very grandioso, just purely as satirical
> and as a counter point; and I copied a great deal from Mr.
> Fred Karno in that direction.[3]

At the age of sixteen, Chaplin started teaching himself to play
violin and cello, and began improvising on piano and organ. He

1. Charles Chaplin, *My Wonderful Visit* (London: Hurst & Blackett, 1922), pp. 92-93.
2. David Robinson, "Chaplin and Music" (1989), *The Songs of Charlie Chaplin* (New
    York: Bourne Co., 1992), p. 18.
3. BBC Light Programme interview with Charles Chaplin, October 15, 1953.

set about taking intermittent lessons, from the theater conductor or from a musician recommended to him. Chaplin played string instruments left-handed, and had his violin and cello strung to accommodate him with the bass bar and sounding post reversed. Although enthusiastic, Chaplin's gifts as a musician were limited (he liked posing with his cello far more than playing it), and realizing that he could never achieve excellence with either instrument, he gave them up in any serious way. Chaplin did, however, play piano and organ adequately and spent hours improvising on these instruments.

In 1916, Chaplin's friend Ben Clark, an English comedian, persuaded Chaplin to go into partnership with him in the music publishing business. Chaplin and Clark rented office space in downtown Los Angeles, and under the banner of the Charlie Chaplin Music Publishing Company, published two songs–"Oh! That Cello" and "There's Always One You Can't Forget"–and the composition "Peace Patrol." Chaplin later dismissed these published works as "very bad."[4]

In 1925, Chaplin published two more songs: "Sing a Song" and "With You Dear, in Bombay." "Sing a Song" was written entirely by Chaplin, and "With You Dear, in Bombay" was composed in collaboration with Abe Lyman and Gus Arnheim. Both songs were recorded by Abe Lyman's California Orchestra.

Although Chaplin's silent films were silent in speech, they were never silent in performance. Silent films were always shown in cinemas with some form of musical accompaniment, at least a piano or an organ or a small ensemble of instruments. Larger cinemas employed scores of musicians to accompany the films. In this way, the "silent film" is a complete and utter misnomer.

Modern filmgoers often have a misconception of the silent film as a scratchy, jumpy, sped-up, slapstick trifle accompanied by a tinkling piano. In reality, silent film performances in the large cinemas of the 1920s were extravagant affairs, complete with crisp, real-time action and magnificently lush and varied musical underscoring complementing the action. And no one understood the power of musical accompaniment to film better than Charles Chaplin, whose instinct for and exposure to music served him well as he began to construct his classic films.

---

4. Charles Chaplin, *My Autobiography* (London: Bodley Head, 1964), p. 243.

Beginning with *A Woman of Paris,* his first film for United Artists, Chaplin worked closely with well-known arrangers to create musical accompaniments that were published and circulated with the first releases of his films. For *The Gold Rush,* Chaplin engaged the musical assistance of Carli Elinor, and for *The Circus,* Chaplin engaged Arthur Kay. The scores for these films were drawn largely from preexisting and popular music in a variety of musical genres, compiling extracts of opera, operetta, incidental music, dance band, and popular tunes of the day.

Chaplin was also an aficionado of classical music and both borrowed from and incorporated entire sequences of classical music into his film scores. Examples of this practice are Chaplin's reworking of Tchaikovsky in *The Kid* and Wagner and Brahms in *The Great Dictator.*

Chaplin's vintage scores to *A Woman of Paris, The Gold Rush,* and *The Circus* went unperformed for nearly seventy years until musicologist Gillian Anderson was invited by the Chaplin family to inventory Chaplin's surviving musical material from the silent era reposited at the Chaplin archives in Corsier-sur-Vevey, Switzerland. Anderson uncovered these premiere scores, and has since performed *The Gold Rush* and particularly *The Circus* to critical acclaim in accompaniment to the films in venues around the world.

Chaplin's suggested scores, however, were not always the accompaniment played to his films when they were shown in the 1920s. Frustrated that he could not control what accompanied his films, Chaplin, who resisted the movement to record dialogue, told a reporter in 1926 that he welcomed the recording of music to accompany a film, undoubtedly in an attempt to receive wider distribution of and control over his musical scores. Chaplin said:

> Music is extremely important . . . that is why I welcome the efforts being made to provide music by mechanical systems, such as the DeForest and the Vitaphone. Mechanical music which has the quality of a symphony orchestra is much better as an accompaniment than feeble vamping on a piano or the excruciating efforts of an incompetent or ill-led orchestra.[5]

When Chaplin prepared the reissue versions of *A Woman of*

---

5. L'Estrange Fawcett, *Films: Facts and Forecasts* (London: Geoffrey Bles, 1930), p. 153.

Paris, The Gold Rush, and *The Circus,* he dismissed the vintage scores he helped prepare in favor of original music that he composed in association with Max Terr (*The Gold Rush*) and Eric James (*The Circus* and *A Woman of Paris*).

Chaplin's composing style is revealed in his own commentary, interviews, and writings of his musical arrangers. Although Chaplin was not a composer in the traditional sense (he was not classically trained in music and could not read or write music), the music that accompanies his films is indelibly his own creation. Although Chaplin lacked the gifts to arrange varied and complex instrumentation, the musical imperative is his, and not a note in a Chaplin musical score was placed there without Chaplin's assent. The experience of each of his arrangers elucidates this subtle distinction.

Chaplin decided to compose an almost entirely original score for *City Lights,* his first film with synchronized sound.[6] Chaplin engaged arranger Arthur Johnson to assist with the composition and arrange the music and described his collaboration with Johnson in this way: "I really didn't write it [the music] down. I la-laed and Arthur Johnson wrote it down, and I wish you would give him credit, because he did a very good job. It is all simple music, you know, in keeping with my character."[7]

Despite this rather modest assessment, Chaplin was explicit with Johnson about what he wanted in the *City Lights* score: "I tried to compose elegant and romantic music to frame my comedies . . . I wanted no competition [between the music and the film], I wanted the music to be a counterpoint of grace and charm . . ."[8]

For the musical accompaniment to *Modern Times,* perhaps Chaplin's finest score, Chaplin enlisted the assistance of a 23-year-old music prodigy named David Raksin. Raksin has given several interviews and has written his own account of his collaboration with Chaplin. His working relationship with Chaplin mirrors the complex give-and-take that defined Chaplin's composing style with his other musical arrangers:

Charlie was generally armed with a couple of musical

6. Chaplin did use some preexisting music in *City Lights,* most notably Padilla's "La Violetera."
7. David Robinson, *Chaplin: His Life and Art* (London: Collins, 1985), p. 412.
8. Charles Chaplin, *My Autobiography* (London: Bodley Head, 1964), p. 355.

phrases ... we would first review the music leading to the sequence at hand and then go on to the new ideas. First, I would write them down; then we would run the footage over and over, discussing the scenes and the music. Sometimes we would use his tune, or we would alter it, or one of us might invent another melody. I should say that I always began by wanting to defer to him; not only was it his picture, but I was working from the common attitude that since I was ostensibly the arranger the musical ideas were his prerogative.[9]

Raksin elaborates even further about his close working relationship with Chaplin:

Charlie and I worked hand in hand. Sometimes the initial phrases were several phrases long, and sometimes they consisted of only a few notes, which Charlie would whistle, or hum, or pick out on the piano ... I remained in the projection room, where Charlie and I worked together to extend and develop the musical ideas to fit what was on the screen ... we spent hours, days, months in that projection room, running scenes and bits of action over and over, and we had a marvelous time shaping the music until it was exactly the way we wanted it.[10]

Herein lies Chaplin's method with respect to each of his arrangers. Chaplin would sing, hum, or pick out musical ideas on the piano. Then his musical arranger would help him flesh out and develop these thoughts. Together they would work and rework the sequences until they were to Chaplin's liking, with Chaplin exercising full authority over each and every note in the score.

Chaplin's next arranger, Meredith Willson (who wrote _The Music Man_), assisted Chaplin in composing the score for _The Great Dictator_, his first full dialogue film. Willson provides a slightly varied account of his working methods with Chaplin and authorized Raksin to quote him regarding the creation of the music for

---

9. David Raksin, "Life with Charlie," _The Quarterly Journal of the Library of Congress,_ Vol. 40, no. 3 (Summer 1983) pp. 234-251.
10. Ibid.

The Great Dictator:

> I know you will want to make it clear that Charlie was a brilliant man, a very creative man. He would come into the studio they had given me to work in, and he would have ideas to suggest—melodies. After that, he would leave me alone. When he came in to see me again I would show him what I was doing, and often he would have very good suggestions to make. He liked to act as though he knew more music than he actually did, but his ideas were very good.[11]

Nevertheless, the music for *The Great Dictator* is ultimately "Chaplinesque" in every way and contains perhaps Chaplin's most haunting pairing of action and classical music: the sequence of Hynkel's balletic dance of world domination with an inflated globe, performed to an arrangement of the prelude to Act I of Wagner's *Lohengrin*. *The Great Dictator* also contains Chaplin's most amusing pairing of action and classical music: the scene of the barber shaving a patron to Brahms's "Hungarian Dance No. 5."

Intimately acquainted with Chaplin's music is composer and conductor Carl Davis, who has reconstructed and performed Chaplin's scores in live accompaniment to his films to large audiences all around the world. Davis provides this perspective on Chaplin's music and working methods:

> For all that one could attack Chaplin's limited knowledge of music, it is amazing—from *City Lights*, the first thing recorded, right to the end—how consistent it is. And of course if it was being written by other people, how is it that the "Chaplin style" maintains itself through widely differentiating and widely changing arrangers? There is a line that goes through, no matter who is working with him. He's saying, "I like it like this," he's humming the tunes, he's making the decisions about the harmonies and orchestrations. There are important lessons in melody and economy to be learned from Chaplin's music.[12]

---

11. Ibid.
12. Carl Davis in an interview with Jeffrey Vance, May 1996.

Chaplin's reliance upon musical associates continued with his later dialogue films. Max Terr assisted Chaplin with the 1942 sound reissue version of *The Gold Rush*; Rudolph Schrager helped Chaplin compose the score for *Monsieur Verdoux*; Ray Rasch was the musical arranger for *Limelight*; and Boris Sarbek collaborated on Chaplin's penultimate film, *A King in New York*.

Tunes extracted from Chaplin's scores emerged as popular songs. His first commercial success was the song "Eternally" from *Limelight* in 1952. The score to *Limelight* is one of Chaplin's finest, including several comic songs and a ballet, "The Death of Columbine."[13] Chaplin's next musical success is his most recognizable song, "Smile," from *Modern Times*. United Artists, pleased with the success of "Eternally," released "Smile" to promote the reissue of *Modern Times* in 1954. United Artists engaged Geoffrey Parsons and John Turner to rework and provide lyrics for the Chaplin melody and recording star Nat King Cole to sing it. "Smile" has become a musical standard and has been recorded numerous times by various artists. Nearly as popular as "Smile" is "This Is My Song" from *A Countess from Hong Kong*, a hit song for which Chaplin wrote the lyrics as well as the music and was first recorded by Petula Clark in 1966.

Chaplin revisited his unscored First National films and UA silent features in earnest for rerelease in the 1970s. Once again, he engaged a musical associate, Eric James, the author of this book, to assist him in his efforts. James had collaborated with Chaplin beginning in 1958 on the reissue of three Chaplin First National films, *A Dog's Life*, *Shoulder Arms*, and *The Pilgrim*, which were rereleased in the compilation film *The Chaplin Revue*. James also worked with Chaplin on the music for his last film, *A Countess from Hong Kong*.

Eric James would assume greater responsibility than Chaplin's previous music arrangers. Chaplin was growing older and relied more heavily on James, particularly for the last scores (*Pay Day*, *A Day's Pleasure*, *Sunnyside*, and *A Woman of Paris*).

Starting with the scoring of *The Circus* in 1968, and continu-

---

13. In 1973, twenty years after its general release, *Limelight* won an Academy Award for best original dramatic score after the film was shown for the first time in Los Angeles and therefore was eligible for the honor.

ing with such films as *The Kid, The Idle Class, Pay Day, A Day's Pleasure, Sunnyside,* and *A Woman of Paris,* Chaplin, now an old man, revisits the music of his youth. The accompaniment that Chaplin created with Eric James for these films reflects the lush, "grandioso" music style of Chaplin's youthful days with the Fred Karno Company. The scores to the feature films *The Circus, The Kid,* and *A Woman of Paris* are saturated with continuous full waves of sound and only the occasional solo.

This accompaniment marks a break for Chaplin from the later style of Gershwin and Porter in the 1920s and 1930s that permeates such Chaplin scores as *City Lights* and *Modern Times,* and the direct cueing that underscores the action of these films. Eric James recalls frequent battling with Chaplin over the 1970s scores to quash Chaplin's insistence on predominately string arrangements. James agrees, however, that Chaplin's 1970s film scores are some of his best work, particularly the music for *The Kid,* which James considers the best score he did with Chaplin.[14]

James, like the earlier Chaplin musical arrangers, was at once recipient of Chaplin's genius, midwife to his muse, and repairer of his musical breach. In the final analysis, the music, however greatly influenced by "musical arrangers," is Chaplin's. Perhaps the best testament to the talent of Chaplin's musical arrangers is the simple and endearing fact that the music they created together remains indelibly and unalterably "Chaplinesque." Thanks to the efforts of Carl Davis, Gillian Anderson, Timothy Brock, and others, live audiences are still enchanted by Chaplin and his arrangers' creations. It is fitting to give the last word on Chaplin and music to his final collaborator, Eric James, whose book assists one greatly in understanding Chaplin's complex and remarkable love affair with music.

Jeffrey Vance
Los Angeles, California
1999

---

14. Eric James in an interview with Jeffrey Vance, March 1999.

Part One

My Early Life

CHAPTER 1

$\mathcal{I}$t was on August 11, 1913, that I came into this world and afterward accepted that the stork had correctly delivered me to a working-class family. Then followed that trial-by-water known as baptism, at a lovely little church standing on the green just the other side of the road from the flat, from which I emerged some time later Eric James Barker, all accomplished without tears, at least on my part.

My mother, until she married at the age of twenty-two, had been in the ranks of that great legalized slave trade known as domestic service. She fetched and carried and waited on every whim of the well-to-do and received from her grateful employers the usual bounty of a few shillings a week, plus an elegant attic room and several hours each night to enjoy it. My father was a carpenter and, except for the period when he served his country in France and Belgium in the First World War, worked all his life in the building department of John Barkers Ltd. of Kensington.

When I was three years old, my father, returning home to England on leave from the front, bought me a toy piano, which he had picked up while passing through central London. A small event in itself, but one which was to have a dramatic effect upon the rest of my life.

By the time he had to return to France, I was able to hit enough right notes for a listener to just recognize "Tipperary." As the months went by, with my mother's encouragement, I added to my repertoire "Keep the Home Fires Burning" and "When Irish Eyes Are Smiling," all these accompanied with singing (my mother questioned if that was the name for it!), in which I used what words I knew, irrespective of their meaning and suitability.

Along with the fascination I expressed for the toy piano was now running an equal fascination for actual printed music. Some of the Sunday newspapers at that time printed music and words of the popular songs. These I would cut out, fold, and keep in my pockets, sometimes solemnly placing one on the toy piano and pretending that I was playing from it, always studying them and never going to bed until I had examined each and every piece. The result of all this was a consensus of opinion among my parents, relatives, and friends that I was showing such an unusual interest in music I should be encouraged in every possible way, not the least by acquiring a real piano.

So, on a morning in July, not long before my fifth birthday, I had the indescribable pleasure of seeing two men, sweating with their exertions and the heat of that summer day, man-handling a piano into the disordered parlor.

It was a poor instrument, costing, as I later learned, £4.10 (four pounds, ten shillings, or $22.50), though that was quite a sum then, especially for those of limited means. I cannot now remember the exact details but I do recall that it had two brass sockets where candle holders should have been and a fretwork front backed with pleated silk, in each of the eight folds with one having a split in it. It had a honky-tonk sound and, when bought, badly needed tuning. Enraptured as I was, I felt like the luckiest and proudest boy in that neighborhood, if not, indeed, the whole world.

The next great event of my life was that which comes to us all, often with a feeling of great trepidation and seldom with any marked enthusiasm—the first day at school. The proprietor was, I was told, a German lady, Miss Stein, with whom I had my first lesson the next day, for she was the one in the school that taught all of us budding pianists. It was the first of many lessons and I came to be regarded as her keenest pupil.

My progress was steadily maintained and very soon I was able to play elementary pieces extremely well. So much did I enjoy playing that every morning before setting off for school, I would practice on the piano at home, much to the annoyance of Mr. and Mrs. Smith, who lived in the flat beneath. They not only hated the noise at that early hour, but also resented the fact that I could and wished to play, while their seven-year-old daughter, Doris, also one of Miss Stein's pupils, showed no liking or aptitude for the piano whatsoever.

My father was, of course, delighted at the progress I was making and he encouraged me all he could and always seemed eager to hear any new piece that I had learned. Life continued placidly and without events of great moment until I was about seven-and-a-half, when it was announced by my mother that Father had found another flat in a more agreeable environment and we were to move ten days later.

Our new home was again an upstairs flat, this time at 27 White Hart Lane, in the South London suburb of Barnes, beautifully situated only two or three hundred yards from the Thames. The towpath, which runs from Barnes Bridge to Mortlake, was only a couple of minutes away and from it one could have a perfect view of the annual Oxford and Cambridge boat race.

Now life was to begin in earnest. An early indication of this was when I arrived at my first real school. It was the Westfield Council school and bore no resemblance whatsoever to Miss Stein's establishment.

I was to prove to be an indifferent scholar, because my heart was not really in anything other than music. I did find arithmetic quite stimulating and actually managed to get prizes in that field, but not for algebra and geometry, which I hated. In spite of my limited academic prowess I did achieve dizzy heights in other directions, because almost as soon as I started at the school I was given the job of playing the piano for the hymn singing during morning prayers.

I had no great love for sporting activities; I went out of my way to avoid them at school, and very seldom joined in the games after school. I much preferred to practice on the piano, study my music books, or read general literature, as I have always been an avid reader.

Shortly after we had made the move, we began to attend the local Anglo Catholic Church of St. Michael and All Angels. My voice having improved considerably, I joined the choir and ultimately became one of the senior boys, not just because of my voice, which although reasonable was not fantastically good, but rather that my ability to read music was such a great advantage.

The time arrived when my parents began to consider the next step in my education. Desiring as always to do the best for me, they wanted to send me to Richmond County School, but could not really afford to do so. However, after a lot of thought and careful budgeting involving personal sacrifices, they finally offered me a choice of either going to Richmond County, or remaining at the Central School and attending the Sheen School of Music every Saturday. The Sheen was a very fine musical academy with excellent teachers and to attend it even part time, concentrating on my one real love, was far more important to me than going to a better school to stuff my head with subjects that would be of no interest or little use in my future career. The decision took one second flat. My parents would have liked to have seen me at the County School for prestige reasons, but they made no effort to persuade me, and once my wishes had been expressed, indicated their happiness for me and their desire to see my efforts prosper.

A very nervous Eric faced the heads of the School of Music for the entry audition, but I apparently pleased them and was accepted because of the standard of playing I had reached. Very soon afterward I was attending separate classes to study the theory of music, an aspect of the subject that I had particularly liked.

I had the tremendous advantage over many musical aspirants because I was born with what is known as "perfect pitch." To explain this simply, it means that one's ears are so attuned that when one hears a sound, one is immediately able to accurately identify and match the note on the piano. It doesn't matter whether the sound is a horn, a bell, or a plucked string, the ear that possesses "perfect pitch" will never lie or fail. Thus, if the teacher played a chord on any part of the piano and asked me to identify the notes in the chord, or discord for that matter, I could immediately do so.

Competitions at the Central Hall, Westminster, were a regular thing in those days and I was always entered and always passed, usually with credit in all that I participated in. Sometimes there would be more than a hundred competing for a prize, and I still cherish the certificates that were awarded to me.

Meantime, I continued as a chorister at St. Michael and All Angels and this aroused my enthusiasm and desire to play the organ, a wish that was translated into action when, under the tuition of Professor Joshua Beswick, I commenced lessons at St. John's Church, Putney.

I had now ceased, after two happy years, to attend the Sheen School of Music and so was free to receive instructions or to practice on the organ every Saturday morning as well as at various other times during the week whenever possible. It was during one session on a Saturday when I was about fourteen-and-a-half years old, that I was confronted by an agitated vicar who said that a dreadful thing had happened. Through a misunderstanding the organist had not turned up to play for a wedding that was due to begin at noon, just half an hour away. The vicar asked if I, for him, or for the love of God or for both, would take the organist's place for the wedding ceremony.

Unfortunately on this Saturday, I was engaged purely in practice and thus not under the personal instruction of Mr. Beswick, so the vicar could not turn to him to deputize. Nervous as I was, I had little choice but to accept the assignment. After that, it was a matter of playing everything in the right place and to pray as I had never prayed before. My prayers were answered, because everything went well, and shortly after I had finished my organ voluntary at the end of the service, the vicar came up to me with warm congratulation and thrust one and a half guineas (£1.11.6 or $8.00) into my hands, "the normal fee" he said, and a reward that I had richly deserved. It was the first real fee that I had ever received and it seemed like a veritable fortune to me. I raced home, highly elated, to receive the plaudits of my parents. I have since regarded this incident as an important milestone in my life, because in one go, it was proven to me that I could earn money from my talents and that I possessed the confidence to perform in front of the public. Soon after this, I was invited to be the regular organist at the Sunday afternoon service at another church, that of All Saints, Putney. I accepted the invitation with eagerness and I remained there for about two years.

In 1928, at the age of fifteen, I reached another and formidable milestone when I left school and had to face the harsh realities of life, standing on my own feet and earning a living.

CHAPTER 2

$\mathcal{W}$hile recognizing the importance of earning a living, I still had to continue my studies and venture deeper into the complexities of music and its interpretations. The next great step that I longed to take was that of playing in an orchestra. To be a soloist is one thing, but to be part of an orchestral team is quite another. I would need some good tuition and I was advised that I could not do better than to attend the special academy adjacent to Westbourne Park Station called the Maud Riseley School for Orchestral Players, and this I did. The first and essential lesson was to absorb the fact that the piano was merely a part of the whole and the player had to subordinate his own feelings and interpretations to a common discipline, and this was not easy. The essential lesson to be learned was that the piano is not normally used in a large orchestra where all various instrumentalists are present. This makes it unnecessary for a pianist to duplicate the various *solo* passages that may have been written by the arranger in the score. It is a cardinal sin to do so and a pianist would very quickly be told in no uncertain terms to leave solos to the musician for whom they had been written. It was tough going but it was not very long before I was sufficiently proficient to be engaged to play with a small orchestra for the dancing sessions at the Hammersmith Ice Rink, now the Palais de Dance.

While pleased to have done it, I was quite glad when the engagement ended, especially as it turned out that another job followed that was to keep me in work for a couple of years. In response to an advertisement, I presented myself at the Savoy Cinema, Uxbridge, where about a dozen other musicians were waiting to audition for the part of organist-pianist. Fortunately for me I was a very quick sight-reader by this time, and this advantage helped me to secure the position against all the rest of the otherwise perfectly efficient applicants.

I have always been very grateful that fate led me to this particular job, because it enabled me to become part of history, as my duties included playing for the silent movies. Without sound of any sort, the need for an imaginative musician to pound out appropriate music to suit the action of the film was absolutely essential. And when one was doing it solo, it was quite a challenge.

In later years when working with Charlie Chaplin, he once turned to me and said, "What did you really think of my early pictures?" I looked at him with a straight face and said, "To tell you the truth Charlie, they gave me a pain in the neck!" A look of astonishment came over his face and for a moment he seemed lost for words. Then he exclaimed, "Well, I'll say this much for you Eric, you're nothing if not honest." Wishing to put him out of his misery as quickly as possible I said, "If you had been sitting playing an Orgapian with your head held back, looking up at a screen, you too would have found your own films a pain in the neck." I went on to explain the job I had done at Uxbridge. At this Charlie began to laugh and continued doing so, interspersing with such comments as "That's a good one, Eric" and "I shall have to tell Oona." He never forgot the incident as it had obviously appealed to an inborn sense of humor that had helped to make him what he was.

My experience at the cinema was invaluable because it taught me to conceive and adapt my musical thoughts very quickly. One had about four musical headings—romantic, dramatic, mysterious, and agitato—and frequently the action of the film demanded a constant to-and-fro between them. In spite of my stiff neck, I enjoyed working there but alas for me—like many thousands of others in the silent film industry—the bright horizon suddenly clouded over when onto the cinema screens of the world burst the new marvel of marvels, the "talkies," and I was out of a job.

I had been earning £3 ($15.00) a week at the cinema, which was a very good wage in those days, especially for a person of my age, and so I was able to save something every week and to be thus able, at the age of 18, to acquire my first car. It was a long time since my previous exciting "first," the piano, and I felt quite proud that between times the piano had enabled me to reach a moment when I could in fact, buy a car. Like the piano, my purchase was of a modest nature and oddly enough the cost—£5 ($25.00)—was virtually the same.

During this period I was taking the odd engagement at various large public houses where, mostly on weekends, they were in the habit of having a pianist play in the lounge bar. I was given these jobs through a brewery firm called Barclay Perkins Ltd., thus I was assured of a modest living. Among the places I played and that I can still remember were the Cock at Sutton, the Surrey Hounds at Caterham, and the Boileau Arms at Barnes. I would play from about 8:00 to 10:30 p.m. with a break of about twenty minutes at 9:00 p.m., and I also had to accompany an artist who was expected to make four appearances in four different acts. I received only £2.10 ($12.50) for each engagement but I was gaining invaluable experience. The artists were necessarily old troupers of the music halls and their music was mostly diabolically written on dog-eared manuscript paper. I must have played appallingly for them sometimes but with the gradual experience that time was giving me I was able to overcome the difficulty of their tatty music sheets and in so doing add another facet to my musical background.

The first step toward a more fulfilling show biz career happened almost by chance. I had gone up to the Archer Street Musicians Club to see if I could pick up any chance gigs but had little success. Feeling in a disconsolate mood, I began to stroll along Brewer Street and into Golden Square. I had never done this before and in retrospect I feel I was being pushed by the hand of fate because I suddenly saw on a brass plate the words "Daniel Mayer Ltd., Theatrical Agents." Without hesitation I entered and climbed the stairs to the first floor where I was confronted by an efficient-looking receptionist, who sweetly inquired if she could help me.

To my surprise I was ushered into an adjacent room where sat a very masculine and awe-inspiring women whose name was Miss Sim Rose. She asked if I could sight read, accompany, and play solos. My immediate reply of "yes" to all these things obviously impressed her, and she asked if I would be interested in joining the cast of a concert party that the company was forming for a summer season at the Esplanade Pavilion, Ryde, Isle of Wight. Would I? My acceptance was immediate. She offered me £5 ($25.00) a week for the thirteen-week season, and I jumped at it. It was a fair remuneration and my first experience in a proper show. I knew I would learn a great deal that would help my future career.

The season confirmed that show biz is not all glamour, and I worked very hard. There were constant rehearsals for the frequent program changes and for my own solo spot. I was both astonished and encouraged by the enthusiastic reception my personal "spot" always received. The applause just carried me to the heights and made it all worth while. It may be a corny thing to say that one gets deep satisfaction from making people happy, but it does.

An old pro once said to me, "Applause won't fill your belly, but if you are a real performer you will find it as essential to life as food and drink." He was so right.

Every Sunday evening there would be a guest artist who had traveled from London for the occasion. I accompanied them all, including the famous baritone Peter Dawson whose voice so moved me. I was thrilled when he went out of his way to compliment me on the way I had accompanied him. The thirteen weeks just flew by and it was soon the sad moment to part from my colleagues, all of whom had contributed so much to establishing my much-needed confidence. I had joined them very much as a new boy, but when I left I was a professional and inwardly I had taken my final solemn vows to devote my life to the stage.

I certainly needed that self-assurance as I made my way back to London to join the swollen ranks of unemployed musicians, doing the Archer Street stomp. Fortunately for me, however, I received a reprieve through a popular bandleader, Lloyd Shakespeare, who had happened to be on the Isle of Wight during my engagement there and had seen the show. He had liked my playing sufficiently to seek me out now and offer me a job with his band during his winter season of West End "gigs" at the principal hotels and similar venues. The money was poor, varying according to hours and finishing time, but it was work. Although I had managed to save £1.10 ($7.50) each of the thirteen weeks I was in the concert party, that would not last long if I were to remain idle. Apart from that I would gain yet more experience and so I gladly took the job. It was hard work and we occasionally did not finish till 2:00 a.m. The routine was that we played throughout the period that dinner was being served, a session that developed into a constant fight; instruments versus PCC (plates, cutlery, and conversation). It was always a battle and alas we seldom won. I sometimes felt we could have played everything backward and it would not have been noticed. After this period we were given a modest free meal in the stewards' room and then back to play nonstop for the cabaret until midnight, 1:00 a.m., or even 2:00 a.m., with no question of a break and no extra payment. The musicians' union had little strength in those days; I must say my "final vows" were under a great strain at times!

My life thus fell into a pattern of playing piano so much that I acquired small corns on the tips of my fingers during the autumn and winter. They only disappeared when I fulfilled my yearly seaside concert party engagement in the summer: Felixstowe, Clacton, and then my greatest achievement, an appointment as conductor for the summer show at the Pier Pavilion, Worthing, for Richard Jerome. Titled "Gay Parade," it might well attract a different kind of audience these days, but in those far off conventional prewar ones, the title conveyed nothing more to those lined up at the box office than that they were in for a cavalcade of happy family entertainment. The Worthing Municipal Orchestra leader, Alex Frankel, was involved in the show and I was privileged to conduct a section of it. I had jumped at the chance and was delighted when I was engaged as pianist-conductor later. After the excitement subsided I had time to ponder on the one little snag that I had somehow forgotten to bring up when I was being considered—I had no experience whatever of conducting!

As the day when I had to do my stuff approached, I began to feel sick at heart. The very idea that I should stand up in front of a bunch of highly experienced musicians, who would quickly be well aware of how green I was, filled me with horror. There are those who will tell you of cases where a conductor has died on the rostrum and the musicians have played on to the end of the piece before noticing the fact! The truth is that individual musicians remain individual musicians without a conductor to bring them together, and I knew what a shambles there would be if I failed to meet at least the minimum technical requirements.

In a highly nervous state I made my way up to the West End to Foyles Book Shop where I purchased a small manual titled "The Art of Conducting." I hurried home and from then it was with me everywhere. I feverishly studied it each waking moment, and when I finally arrived at the pier my confidence was so high that I felt Sir Henry Wood could look to his job now that I was about! Alas, overconfidence is a poor companion, and when I stepped down after the first rehearsal and walked toward Alex Frankel, I was at once brought back to earth when he took me to one side and said, "Half my lads will be down with pneumonia if you keep creating such a draught with your impression of a windmill." I looked crestfallen and he continued so quietly and politely to explain that I was waving my arms about as if conducting a symphony orchestra and the dozen musicians could virtually follow the beat from the disturbance of the air without bothering to look up. Far better to conduct in an imaginary small box and so compel the musicians to watch the baton. This was invaluable advice and I have used it since, especially whenever a tight accompaniment with an artist or instrumentalist is virtually essential. I owe a lot to that bunch of fellows for their indulgence and kindness. I resolved that whenever I was a member of an orchestra, I would never make things difficult for a conductor.

It was a hard show for me. I had to score almost every item of music and spent night after night, after the show had finished, preparing the various parts that the orchestra needed the next morning. At the end of the season I returned to London and took up again with Lloyd Shakespeare and commenced doing gigs all over the place.

Apart from theaters, there was also an abundance of work to be had in the world of after-dinner entertainment. There were no fewer than twelve hundred Masonic Lodges meeting in the greater London area at least eight times a year, as well as private functions, company dinners, and Masonic Ladies Night Balls. This meant that for good solo artists (singers, entertainers, comedians, and pianist accompanists) there was always a constant supply of work. It should be mentioned that most Masonic Lodges had their own organist who would accompany the artists and it was accepted that the choice of songs would always be influenced by his ability to play them, thus limiting the artist to performing songs in the simple keys of C, G, and F.

At the numerous seaside resorts around the coast of Great Britain, there were pierrots or concert parties, which consisted of six or seven artists with varying degrees of vocal or visual talent entertaining the holiday makers for anything between three to five months, depending on the venue. Blackpool, Scarborough, Ayr, Great Yarmouth, Brighton, and Eastbourne were generally recognized as the resorts that could offer the longest season's work. Many of those at the end of the summer engagement "filled in" with after-dinner work and frequently in the winter went into pantomime, which was also a most popular form of entertainment in the larger towns and cities. Among the many hotels and banqueting rooms that existed in London's West End were the Savoy, Grosvenor House, Dorchester, Ritz, Piccadilly, Great Eastern, Charing Cross, Park Lane, Rembrandt, Café Royal, Holborn Restaurant, and the largest of all, the Connaught Rooms, where there were at least twenty banqueting rooms and the facilities to cater for more than two thousand guests every night of the week. A common practice among artists who happened to be "resting" was for them to go clad in evening dress and wander along the corridors of the Connaught Rooms in the ever likely possibility that an artist would be unable to perform for some reason or other. They would immediately be engaged "on the spot" by the lodge organist to appear for him at the function for which he was responsible.

So the hard graft continued and I decided it would be a financially sound idea to get a regular daytime job. In 1937 I went up to London's West End to Tin Pan Alley (Denmark Street) for an interview at the Sun Music Publishing Co., a subsidiary of the great Francis, Day & Hunter Co. The interview was successful and I was assigned to the professional department as a song plugger. In those days the most satisfactory way to popularize a song was to secure "plugs" on radio and recordings. This was done by personal contact with the various name artists most likely to feature the songs in question. My own particular assignment in the plugging game was to make personal calls to the various theaters and music halls in the greater London area, or to the cinemas that were featuring cine-variety. There I would speak to the star artists in which we were interested.

It was a very happy time for me and I met many artists, both well known and less so. I would take them into a small room and play over the songs on which we were currently working. I recall one young lady, most likeable but a little shy, who came in and sang the song to such effect that I was moved to tell her that I thought that one day she would be a big star; she laughed and said "I bet you say that to all the girls." I replied that with all the singers I dealt with I was in a good position to recognize something special when it came my way. I added, rather pompously perhaps, "you have stardust on your shoulders." She laughed even louder and retorted, "It's probably dandruff dear, but thanks all the same."

She got up and Vera Lynn walked slowly along the corridor to a future greater than even I could have foretold.

On another occasion, Larry Adler came in a great state of agitation; apparently he had just been rehearsing with the orchestra at the London Palladium a program that included his own fabulous arrangement of Gershwin's "Rhapsody in Blue"; unfortunately things had not gone well, so he had rushed over to our office to see if there was by any chance a pianist capable of accompanying him in his rendering of this special piece. By sheer coincidence I had recently been practicing that very composition and I knew it backwards. I played it through for him and he was delighted. On the spot he explained the sections he would be using. We had a couple of run-throughs and I returned with him to the Palladium where I played for him that very night. The following three weeks we did two shows a night and it was, for me, a most thrilling and stimulating assignment. I was, of course, excused from all plugging for that period and I had to get deputies for my other gigs. But it was worth it, both to accompany the world's greatest harmonica player and to appear at the Palladium. Following this we did several cabaret engagements in the West End and also a number of recordings at the HMV studios.

I had been at Francis, Day & Hunter Co. about a year when I heard that the position of professional manager was available at the Southern Music Publishing Co., which was also established in Tin Pan Alley, just around the corner. I went after the post and got it. As this change carried with it an increase in salary it meant my financial problems would be greatly eased. Life continued much the same, the usual evening gigs and the plugging at other times.

I continued happily as professional manager of the Southern Music Co., plugging away like mad and sufficiently keen to always carry a small portable gramophone, plus handle, so that I could at any time play the appropriate American recordings to any star I encountered. That seemed to impress quite a few people and many of them would visit me in my office in order that I might play and sing my plugged numbers. One such visitor, a big star named Elsie Carlisle, was to have a great effect upon my life. When she came to me she was still convalescing after a long illness and was in fact escorted by a nurse she introduced as Leila O'Dwyer. Elsie Carlisle's illness had been front-page news and some papers had carried a daily bulletin. The Westminster City

Council had taken the unusual step of spreading a large amount of straw on the road outside her house, 8 Deanery Street, Park Lane, Mayfair, in order to lessen the noise of the passing traffic. It was a most unusually compassionate act to come from a local government office and serves to illustrate the genuine concern felt by everyone. Thanks to the treatment of a Harley Street specialist, she was able to avoid surgery, though the illness was long and expensive. She was thus eager to recommence her career, hence her appearance in my office. She was looking for a pianist to accompany her during the many recordings she was due to make at Decca Studios with the "house" orchestra, conducted by Jay Wilbur. I offered myself for the job and as she liked my work I was duly engaged, and not very long afterward I was engaged yet again, this time to Elsie's nurse Leila, who I subsequently married. Elsie, her young brother, Willie, and her son, Harry, became very good friends of mine, so together with Leila, Elsie's visit to my office had brought four people into my life.

I left the Southern Music Co. early in 1939 and was thus free to accompany Elsie Carlisle to the various music hall engagements all over the country. As this work did not guarantee that I would be engaged every week I had to look around for a more regular source of income. I was offered an engagement starting in the early summer at Cliftonville, a seaside holiday resort near Margate, on the southeast coast of Great Britain. Thus it was that in June of that year I commenced a fifteen-week summer season with the Oval Entertainers at the Oval Bandstand, which was in the center of a two-thousand-seat arena. We performed twice daily; when the weather was good it was most enjoyable but when it took a turn for the worse it could be tough, especially when the wind got up. On these occasions I think that the sight of the company doing their acts while holding onto the props and me clutching my music and playing the piano with one hand got as many laughs as the show itself.

We all needed laughs, both performers and the large audiences we continued to attract, as over our conclave, as over all of Britain, a stronger and more chilling wind was blowing. We did our stuff, the audiences responded, children ran about with their ice creams, others rode on donkeys, people bathed, sat on the sands and indeed behaved as holiday makers always have. However, somehow it all seemed so much more intense, as if everyone was trying to extract the very last microcosm of enjoyment out of their holiday.

There was a tension in the air that one could almost feel; the laughter was more abandoned, the applause almost excessive. Superficially everything was the same but just under the surface lay the fears that few wished to express, that this would be the last holiday for many years, perhaps forever. This almost fanatical preoccupation with the need to be happy ensured a very successful run for our show and both audience and performers seemed to be bonded by a feeling of companionship and understanding such as I had never known before. By the end of August the news left us in little doubt that we were on the brink of an abyss and it was with heavy hearts that we began our evening show on Saturday, September 2nd. The next morning Mr. Chamberlain, the prime minister, announced that we were at war and for us the show was over; the curtain was now rising on a new production in which there would be very few laughs.

Slowly, one by one, the members of the troop departed back to their rooms to pack and head for home. We all shook hands and swore eternal friendships. Suddenly it was all over and I was heading disconsolately toward London. The constant stream of army vehicles with their guns, searchlights, and equipment heading toward the place from whence I had come emphasized the reality of a situation that had seemed hitherto too enormous to comprehend.

CHAPTER 3

After a few days back in London without the immediate dramatic conflagration for the nation that had been anticipated, it was apparent that life would be continuing much the same for at least a time, and that the closing of theaters along the vulnerable coast line did not apply to those more inland. As a result I rejoined Elsie Carlisle and began a tour around the various music halls that were still functioning. The first tangible evidence was that one had to register for military service, and I applied for the Royal Air Force where I hoped to become a wireless operator. A few months later, during the summer of 1941, Elsie was engaged to do a radio series called "Carlisle Express" to be recorded at the BBC studios in Bristol.

By early September we had reached the final program and we were in fact rehearsing for it, when I was informed by the commissionaire that two gentlemen wished to see me. The taller of the two, with an undisguised look of pleasure at my discomfort, addressed me in a voice designed to reach the ears of those in the most distant part of the building. "Contrary to the provisions of the Armed Forces and Defense of the Realm Act 1939, you failed to respond to the notice of enlistment assigning you to Royal Air Force Cardington or to subsequent communications. Accordingly you are to accompany us immediately, and you are advised to do so peacefully for your own sake." The shock was petrifying and I could only stammer out that I had never received anything. Boot faced, they told me to get my coat. Only the intervention of Elsie and the producer, who pointed out that I was engaged in a recording for a show that would go out nationwide, finally persuaded them to let me stay and report next day to RAF Cardington in Bedford. I was very shaken up by the event and by the fact that my professional life with all its commitments was to be terminated at a stroke without warning.

The next day I drove up to Cardington and was duly taken in to the presence of Flight Lt. Narbeth, who greeted me rather belligerently with, "So you are the man we have searched all over England for." Foolishly perhaps I retorted that I was flattered to be considered so important. His reaction was anything but friendly and I had to talk fast and furious to convince him that I really had not received my call-up papers. I put forward the possibility (confirmed many years later) that the papers may have gone to the comedian Eric Barker who, with his wife Pearl Hackney, did so much broadcasting. I also pointed out that I was up to my eyes in work that gave pleasure and comfort to people throughout Britain, both military and civilian, via the BBC, and that it was unreasonable to expect me to drop everything and for the BBC to replace me.

The officer suggested that I take ten days from my annual leave entitlement of twenty-eight days. I thanked him profusely and offered to organize a show for his RAF unit absolutely free. This pleased him and we parted on considerably better terms than I would have previously thought possible. So for the next few days I was busy fulfilling engagements and making arrangements to have the future work to which I was committed taken over by other artists. I was also able, during these few days prior to enlisting, to give serious thought to the war effort and the role that I was to play in it.

On the appointed day I drove up to Cardington in my old Vauxhall saloon and reported for duty at the forbidding looking guardroom. I found myself in a Nissen hut with forty other blokes. As I lay in bed swathed in a permanent fog of smoke and sweat I resolved to get to hell out of it at the first opportunity. The following morning we were outfitted and I at once called on Narbeth and told him I was all set to put on the concert I had promised. He was quite excited at this and said I would be given every assistance.

I grabbed at this like a drowning man and told him how impossible it would be to organize anything when I was stuck in a hut with dozens of others and no phone to call artists all over the country. Could I therefore be excused after final parade each day and be allowed to drive to nearby Bedford where I would set up headquarters at the Bridge Hotel. He swallowed hard but agreed and so I was able to return to civilization each evening, enjoy a good dinner and relax in the comfort of a nice hotel. By the end of the second week I had organized and presented a really good show starring Elsie Carlisle and the comedian Max Bacon, ably supported by the three Calores sisters and several others. It was a roaring success.

I had by this time applied for a wireless operators course and the postings were to take place in a few days. The course was held both at Morecombe and Blackpool, and when I told Elsie she was overjoyed because she was appearing the following week at the Palace Theatre Blackpool and desperately needed me. Without further ado she approached the senior officer and explained how important it was that my posting should be to Blackpool. He began to huff and puff a bit but she put her hand on his shoulder, ruffled his hair a bit and said, "Come on, be a good boy, it can't make any difference to you and I will be so grateful." I stood hoping that the ground would open and swallow me up but to my astonishment he just said, "Happy to oblige you Miss Carlisle," and that was that.

The following morning I asked to see him and explained that I must take my car with me and if I took two or three other airmen at the same time and drove to Blackpool, could I have the cost of the rail tickets to help toward petrol. For a moment he just regarded to me with a glassy stare. Furiously drumming his fingers on the desk he at last blurted out, "You must try and understand Barker that we are transferring over three hundred men, not just you, and if you want to keep out of trouble in the RAF you're going to have to learn to conform." I stood my ground and he seemed to sense that I was not going to give in easily. He suddenly roared, "Why the hell is it so important that you should have your car?" I explained that I had an excessive amount of baggage, including music, and I needed special facilities. His finger-drumming increased and then he stretched out his hand for the phone, rang the station, and arranged for a transporter wagon to be hitched to the train. I thanked him profusely, saluted smartly, and left the office. Thus it was that aircraftman Eric Barker took his car with him on the journey to the north and drove it off some six hours later to Blackpool.

Not only had I achieved the impossible but before leaving I was handed a letter addressed to the adjutant, RAF Blackpool, in which this same indulgent officer requested that I be accorded whatever facilities were needed to enable me to play nightly at the Palace Theatre. I now realized that life in the RAF would be a good deal less horrific than I had feared, and my transfer to Blackpool was to confirm my good fortune. I was accommodated with four other airmen at a modest house in Palatine Road that, although by no means comparable to the Bridge Hotel in Bedford, was made a happier place because of the efforts of Mr. and Mrs. Alderson, an elderly Yorkshire couple whose house it was and who were so kind, tolerant, and generous. They fed us well, if simply, and all for the official rate of £1.7.6 ($8.00) a week per person. When I was interviewed by Pilot Officer Tommy Elliot, who, it transpired, was a great fan of Elsie Carlisle, he didn't hesitate in giving me the okay to appear each night at the Palace Theatre. I was so grateful that I at once offered to get together a really first class show for the airmen in Blackpool. He was very pleased, because it had long been a sore point that the town, in spite of its many theaters, could not meet the needs of 100,000 airmen plus the civilian population.

He offered any help he could give and I suggested straight away that I might be permitted to see in advance the manifestos of the future intake, so that I might pick out the professional artists among them. Before very long the lists produced such people as the arranger/pianist Norrie Paramor, drummer Lou Jacobson, violinist Lew Whiteson, comedian Max Wall, and many, many others, including my pianist friend Harry Engleman. When he turned up I suggested to the adjutant that it might help if Harry and I were to occupy the "digs" in Palatine Road, exclusively, especially as there was a piano there that would be ideal for practice undisturbed by other occupants. It was like rubbing Aladdin's lamp, because by the following day Harry had moved in and the others were moved out, and there, no matter what happened around us, Polish, English, WAAFs coming and going all the time, aircraftmen Engleman and Barker stayed put at No. 30 for three years.

So, with this first hurdle overcome, I went off to begin the agonizing few weeks of irritation that every newly arrived airman has to go through. This included a medical examination from which I was judged unsuitable for aircrew due to bad eyesight and was therefore allocated to general duties.

When one morning we were marched off to the Winter Gardens Ballroom to be given an intensive course of drill and exercises I was horrified and my misery was increased when I saw that the number of airmen were far too great even for that very large hall. When we were lined up we were far too close to each other. The instructor informed us that we were the greatest shower of debilitated humanity that he had ever had the misfortune to see and that he was going to put some life into us if it was the last thing he did. He then proceeded to demonstrate the sequence of exercises that he expected us to perform, which included swinging both arms fully extended, similar to the breast stroke in swimming, and jumping at the same time. He went on to say that when we heard him shout "Commence" it would be followed by more instructions, but the rest was never heard. Half of the assembled company of airmen decided that this was the moment to commence the exercises just shown them, and before his voice had died away in the ensuing bedlam, the hand of the man next to me delivered a stinging blow to my face, sending my spectacles flying. I shook my head to get rid of the stars and turned round just in time to see the foot of another man land squarely on them. He removed his foot to disclose a little heap of broken glass and twisted metal.

I groped my way out of the building and somehow found my way to Tommy Elliot's office, where I charged in and told him in no uncertain manner that I was not prepared to have to pay £10 ($50.00) for a new pair of spectacles every time I had to do this stupid physical training business. He eyed me with scarce disguised amusement and, without a word, picked up a pad and wrote on it, "This man is excused all drill and P.T. until further notice," signed Pilot Officer T. Elliot. I turned toward the door still somewhat disgruntled when he called me back. "Now that we have cleared the way, what about the show you promised?" I returned and sat down at his invitation. "What do you need to get started?" he asked.

I peered toward him through the haze of my short sightedness and retorted sharply, "A new pair of glasses." He leaned back in his chair, clicked his fingers and I said, "Worry not, I'll need an office, I must have somewhere to keep all the paperwork." "Shall do," he said, making a note. "I'll need a phone or a runner." He blinked but made a note, "Shall do, anything else?" "At the moment, no, but later I'll need volunteers, pressed or otherwise to work backstage. I'll confirm details later."

I left the office blessing the foot that had found my spectacles. Before another day was out I had my office, on the door of which my opening hours were clearly marked, 9:00 a.m.–12:30 p.m. and 2:00 p.m.–5:00 p.m. each day, and Saturday morning 9:00 a.m.– noon.

Unfortunately, there was no telephone in the room allocated to me at the time and as it was essential that I should be able to get in touch with potential performers for the upcoming shows, I would have to contact them by letter. Sending them by post would not be practical and so I requested the services of airmen who would act as couriers. There was a long bench in the office and there was always a continuous supply of airmen sitting on it awaiting my instructions to deliver correspondence all over Blackpool. Not five minutes in the RAF, just a common airman and yet I had an office with never less than six recruits to do my bidding. Service life was getting better by the minute. I sometimes smile when I think back and remember how many of these newly conscripted airmen used to salute me in the mistaken impression that I was an officer!

My first show was held in the four-hundred-seat Jubilee Theatre, whose directors had very kindly agreed to let us have the use of it one evening each alternate week. There was no shortage of volunteers, including the wives of three corporals who undertook to organize the refreshments for the artists. I considered it to be so important to treat them as well as we could as they were giving their services completely without payment of any kind. I was able to keep up a good standard of refreshments thanks to some of the patriotic stallholders in the market who regularly contributed a supply of the essential food items without insisting on such mundane things as coupons.

Although still running my car, I had an account with the local taxi driver named Dyson who boasted amongst his vehicles a large Rolls Royce, absolutely ideal for collecting and returning artists who had so kindly appeared in the shows to their respective theaters.

About this time my friend Harry Engleman and I created a dual piano act, "The RAF's Flying Fingers." We had discovered two upright pianos at Sharples, the local music shop, where we were able to formulate the two-piano arrangements of the music best suited to us. We appeared fortnightly in our regular show, which incidentally we called "Flight." We proved very popular with the audience who, because of our rather stout proportions, had retitled "Flying Fingers" to "Flying Fortresses" when referring to us. They were so enthusiastic with our performances that we decided to contact the Air Ministry and offer to do broadcasts for the forces overseas. They were delighted, and so we traveled to London about once every three months to record four fifteen-minute broadcasts.

During the three years I was in Blackpool I was able to fulfil quite a number of engagements with my old friend Elsie Carlisle whenever she came within "striking distance." I can truthfully say that during that period of time I played every theater or music hall in a fifty-mile radius: Liverpool, Preston, Morecombe, Manchester, Oldham, Ashton-under-Lyne, Blackburn, Bolton, and Blackpool, of course.

A time was reached during the war when things were going really badly for Britain and her allies; every news bulletin and newspaper reported strategic withdrawals, redeployment of forces and other such official jargon that, translated, meant that we were being knocked for six all over the place. It got to a point where the outlook was so bleak that only Churchill's brilliant performances propped up the nation's flagging spirits. The magnitude of the crisis was brought home to me when an Air Ministry directive commanded that all members of the permanent staff, including us entertainment "wallahs," had to learn to use a rifle.

Our instruction on the rifle followed quickly on the directive and we were taken to Bispham from where we had to march to the Rossall firing range. As Harry had flat feet and I was a poor marcher, we were put in front of the squad to set the pace. After a while we came to a large dip, virtually a hole in the road; we thought it odd but marched down it, along and up the other side only to find on looking back that there was not a soul behind us. We turned, retraced our steps and rejoined the squad just as they arrived at the range. They had a good laugh at our expense and we learned that it was a put up job: the warrant officer had whispered "right turn" and we had just trudged along talking and completely in a world of our own.

When our turn came to shoot we lay our rotund bodies on to the groundsheets and we examined our rifles with suspicion and perplexity. We were shown how to put in the clip of five cartridges, which meant using force against the return spring. Harry immediately rebelled and said he was a professional pianist and was not going to risk his fingers in that contraption. So there and then before the unbelieving gaze of the instructor he pushed them in with his ballpoint pen. It was a godsend the German High Command never got to know about it! I loaded in the normal way with complete disregard to the consequences. Harry said I was just trying to get a medal. The instructor, swallowing hard, yelled "Fire at will"; Harry started to say, "Which is Will," but I hissed him and suggested we got on with it. He at once closed his eyes and pressed the trigger and then let out a yell as the recoil banged the rifle into his shoulder. "Reload and carry on," shouted the instructor and Harry proceeded to do so with eyes tightly closed and a yelp of pain between each shot until all five had gone.

By this time I was also blazing away but sweating so much that my glasses steamed over and I was firing blind as well. When the last sounds of our volleys had died away flags began to wave from all parts of the "butts," not just above our target. For a moment we thought the king had turned up, but the instructor explained in unprintable adjectives that all the flags indicated a complete miss with every shot and the unofficial white one was probably put up by a frightened "butt" orderly as an indication that he was prepared to surrender. We were told later that a prize bull standing three fields away ended up unfit for anything but slaughter, but this was never confirmed. Funnily enough, in spite of the Air Ministry directive, we were never asked to fire a rifle again.

As if we hadn't had enough aggravation for one day we were faced with more on the way back. Harry and I were in the usual head of column position setting the same casual marching pace when we became aware of Cpl. Jack Smitten bellowing, "Left, right, left, right," more suited to the style of the Brigade of Guards than a shower of permanent staff "erks," for whom walking at all was a hard enough exercise. I yelled to the corporal, "If you don't march at the tempo of which we are capable we won't march in your rotten squad at all." His face hardened and he said, "Right, you two are on a charge," and then he began to shout "left, right" even louder. "That's it," said Harry and we slowed down to a strolling pace.

The result was inevitable. The first rank behind us hit against us and the next rank against them and so on down the line. Goodness knows how it would have ended had not a miracle happened in the shape of Mr. Dyson driving his Rolls Royce toward us. As he drew level I shouted "Dyson"; he yelled back "Sir" and pulled up immediately. As we climbed inside I told the corporal that we'd had enough and would see him back at the office. With the whole squad, including corporal, standing with open mouths, we swept past them sitting comfortably in the back of this beautiful limousine and rode happily back into Blackpool. We went at once to see the adjutant and had hardly left when a very irate Cpl. Smitten arrived and was ushered into the office, there to complain bitterly about our behavior. He was quietly dealt with and nothing further came of it.

I am sure that the reader will by now have concluded that there were two Air Forces in Britain at that time. The Royal Air Force and the Blackpool Air Force, two distinct bodies of men of whom any similarity was purely accidental; Fred Karno (the producer of the internationally famous "Mumming Birds Revue" that Chaplin and his half brother Sydney toured with in the early 1900s) could scarcely have done better. I could give hundreds of incidents if I had the space. The example of Cpl. Alex Munro of 9 RC (Recruiting Center) illustrates it perfectly. As a corporal, his job was to put the "rookies" through sessions of square bashing, which means drilling on a parade ground. Universal military terms are used all over the world and one is the command "halt" when a squad of men is required to come to an immediate standstill. This is usually followed by another, which will be either "Squad—right turn" or "Squad—left turn."

This particular corporal devised his own set of commands such as "Squad—STOP" or "Squad—face the way I'm facing." When they were expected to be on parade at 7:30 a.m., the window on the first floor of the front of his quarters would open and standing there in what appeared to be his uniform would be Cpl. Alex Munro, who would take a roll call to check that all in his squad were present. After a few commands he would shout, "Squad—piss off, I'll see you at the pool table saloon at ten o'clock," and then he would remove his RAF greatcoat and go back to bed for another hour. The men loved it but he was constantly being censured by his superiors.

Another corporal who was later to achieve great fame in show business was Cpl. Max Wall. Unlike Munro, he strove for perfection to such a degree that he was far from popular. Oddly enough the rookies respected him and as each squad finished their initial training there was always a collection to buy a small gift for him.

Meantime I continued to devise and produce "Flight" at the Jubilee Theatre. It was during one of these performances that Wall created his very famous character. In all seriousness an announcement was made from the stage that I was unfortunately indisposed and would be unable to appear with Harry Engleman for the double piano act; it was gratifying to hear a crescendo of "aaah" and one or two cries of "shame," but the emcee lifted up his hands and then announced that they had been lucky enough at the last minute to secure the services of the world famous concert pianist, Professor Wallofski. Max then came on and gave a hilarious performance, with Harry's assistance, of Liszt's Hungarian Rhapsody; it brought the house down and had us all in stitches. From then on Max was obliged, by popular demand, to include it in every one of his stage performances while in the RAF and since then has repeated it in theaters all over the world, even during an ice show in London.

My adjutant friend Tommy Elliot had by now been promoted and had become my commanding officer, which made things even easier, if that were possible. One favor he did me was to allow a delayed weekend pass on a Tuesday and Wednesday for six consecutive weeks in order that I might drive across to Bangor in North Wales to play for Elsie Carlisle and look after her musical arrangements for the broadcasts. At this time the BBC programs were almost entirely recorded or broadcast from there. The BBC Variety Orchestra, under its conductor Charles Shadwell, was resident in the town and I got on splendidly with them, but it never occurred to me for one moment that I would one day actually be a member of this famous orchestra.

In 1943 my very good friend and the superstar of many of my shows, Max Wall, finally paid the price for his untiring efforts and standards of perfection both as a performer and RAF instructor. He put his heart and soul into both jobs and it gave him an anxiety neurosis that landed him in a psychiatric hospital and subsequent discharge with honor from the service. It was a great blow to me to lose such a popular artist whose dedication was absolute; I shall always be grateful to him. Fortunately he quickly recovered and by and by was able to use his great talent to entertain people all over the British Isles and continued to do so until his death.

Another and even greater shock occurred when Harry and I were on one of our regular trips to London. We had done the recordings and gone our separate ways, Harry to Birmingham and I to Barnes, where as I approached my home I anticipated with pleasure relaxing and exchanging all the news with my parents. As I made to turn into Brookwood Avenue I found my passage barred by a rope across the road and my eyes stared in shocked disbelief at the sight of absolute devastation. At least half of the houses were completely destroyed or very seriously damaged and every other house had received damage of some sort. I felt physically sick and I turned and leaned on the hood of my car in a state of paralyzed incomprehension; minutes before my mind had been full of the happy anticipation of relaxing in the sitting room, chatting with my parents over a cup of tea; now even the cup I might have drunk from was probably smashed to fragments and as for my mother and father, I just tried to shut them from my mind for I dare not even contemplate the horrific possibilities. I was suddenly aware that a warden had come over to talk to me. He was able to tell me that my mother was in hospital with a head injury plus cuts and bruises but not in any danger, and my aunt Carrie, who was staying with my parents, and Mr. Champion, an elderly lodger, had escaped with injuries not serious enough for them to be taken to hospital. My father had thereafter cause to be thankful for his long, practiced habit of visiting the Manor Arms for a quick drink each night after leaving Barker's, so mercifully he was not at home. Though of course he was as shocked as I was when he arrived there and found only the front of the house still standing.

I saw my mother in hospital and did all I could to help, and then I had to return to Blackpool where a further shock awaited me. My friend and commanding officer Tommy Elliot called me into his office and told me that our whole unit, which incidentally was known as "Suspendair," an abbreviation for "Suspended air crew," was to be moved. He told me in confidence that we were going to the air base at Eastchurch on the Isle of Sheppey. He also very kindly offered to arrange for me to stay in Blackpool so that I might continue my activities in entertainment. On the face of it, it might seem madness not to have accepted but I have a strong sense of loyalty and friendship and I nobly announced that I was not going to desert him just because things were getting tougher. He was obviously delighted at my gesture and I set about winding things up in Blackpool.

Finally the day dawned when we arrived at Eastchurch, a very old aerodrome that today continues to be used but as a civilian open prison; some might consider that no change! When I beheld the cold and bleak huts, the forlorn NAAFI Building and absorbed the fact that the sum total of off-duty places of relaxation was one little pub in the small village a mile up the road, I began to regret the virtuous feelings that had prompted me to reject Tommy's offer. I therefore made application to see Tommy and he agreed that I had made a mistake in not stopping in Blackpool. He was quite genuinely sorry at the way things had turned out but said that he would take steps right away to have me remuster to my accredited trade in the RAF Manual, to wit an ACH/musician (aircraft hand/musician).

Within two weeks I was on my way to Uxbridge to join the ranks of other musicians at the RAF camp under Wing Commander O'Donnell. I soon settled down to the easygoing routine to which I had been formerly accustomed. The day started at 9:00 a.m. with a parade and we were dismissed at noon. For three weeks this happy state of affairs continued until I was suddenly summoned to O'Donnell's office, there to be told that I was posted to Records, Gloucester, beginning the following Monday. At the mere mention of the word "records" cold shivers ran up and down my spine and I went weak at the knees. To anyone serving in the RAF to be sent to "Records" is on a par with Russian soldiers being sent to Siberia. O'Donnell agreed that it was as big a mystery to him as it was to me, but that he had no choice as it was a name posting, so I and I alone had to go.

The following Monday, I set off to a place called Barnswood on the outskirts of Gloucester. On arrival I was escorted very quickly through an enormous building to a huge office labeled "Bomber Command." Eventually I arrived at a large desk where sat Flight Lt. Eldred. By now I was seething inside and ready to complain bitterly at having been so un-ceremoniously moved, but his opening words and his considerate approach disarmed me immediately. "Sit down Barker," he said, "and I sincerely hope that you won't take umbrage after you have heard what I have to say." He leaned back in his chair, smiled and said, "The fact is, your fame as a producer of shows has at last reached this benighted spot; a friend of yours, Tubby Clark (pilot officer) has recently arrived here from Blackpool and has been singing your praises to such an extent that the C.O. was determined to get you here and try to persuade you to present similar shows for this establishment." As I sat there feeling quite taken aback, he went on to explain that there were four thousand WAAFs and one thousand airmen on the station, all of them working hard at tedious repetitive work and never finishing their duties until at least 6:00 p.m. By the time they had had a meal and cleaned up they would arrive in Gloucester too late to find seats at the various cinemas and theaters; this was bad for morale, especially as most seats went to the thousands of civilians working in the numerous factories in and around the area. Would I therefore please undertake the production and presentation of shows for the RAF alone?

This unexpected outcome to my unwanted posting was quite a shock and I realized that I could hardly refuse the invitation. Thankfully, surprised as I was at the outcome of this interview, I retained possession of my wits and so found myself agreeing to do as I was asked, subject only to certain conditions. For me, comfort and privacy always having been of top priority, I requested private "digs" outside the confines of the camp. I then explained that I was frequently called upon to do broadcasts for the services and that I must continue to be granted the facilities to do them as and when they occurred. My third condition was that funds would have to be made available to cover running expenses, such as costume hiring, talent competition prizes, and so on. I went on to explain that in order to secure the voluntary services of possible performers in this RAF station we would have to hold talent contests with modest prizes of money. Finally, I brought up the question of transport to and from my housing, as whatever the distance would certainly be more than I would wish to walk twice a day.

When I had finished laying down the details of my ultimatum, I wondered how soon I would be on my way back to Uxbridge! However, within seconds the officer pressed a button thus summoning a warrant officer who was instructed to find me the best billet in Gloucester. He thought for a minute and then said that it was without doubt a Mr. and Mrs. Chater at 11 Reservoir Road but that it was already occupied by an RAF sergeant. Without hesitation, Eldred clicked his fingers and said, "Have him removed at once." He then looked down at his notes and said, "Your broadcast commitments, that's OK—funds to cover expenses—that's OK." I staggered away to begin my new RAF career, still unable to believe that the demands of a common airman could have been met without a quibble.

The very next day a meeting was called at which I was formally introduced to a group of officers who were all willing to give their time and efforts to the task of bringing the entertainment project into being. Group Captain Jones, the senior officer, who was an extremely able and likeable man, pledged his support all along the line.

The name "Off the Record" was quickly established as an ideal title for the shows and preparations were soon under way. Selfridges were kind enough to give me a very good deal on a Grand Piano, which they duly delivered to the Concert Hall. There was a very talented Station Orchestra under the control of Sergeant Norman Petchey, who was an enormous help to me. The orchestra acted in an accompanying capacity but at times a section of it would be featured as an independent act; there was also a string quartet in which the Group Captain's Wife, P/O Ena Jones, played the cello. Talent competitions were held throughout the camp with the aid of Frank Eldred and the Education Officer Flight Lt. Etheridge and modest money prizes were given for best talent. This resulted in several amateurs justifying a spot in the shows. Luckily we had an ex-professional dancer among the Station WAAFs and she was able to find seven other girls to provide the necessary glamour. Thus, under Flying Officer Molly Parker, a group was organized who performed under the title "The WAAF Tappers." Meanwhile a draft note was sent to Blackpool to post in Cpl. Alex Horsburgh, otherwise known as Alex Munro. Apparently, when it arrived, Alex was playing a game of snooker with the C.O. W/Commander Ranson. The game was immediately abandoned in order to organize opposition to the posting and even the Air Officer Commanding of Blackpool himself, Air Commodore Howard Williams, was asked to intervene. But his efforts and all the signals that flashed feverishly backward and forward were all to no avail. Nobody, but nobody could ever win against Records Gloucester.

Three weeks later I was at Gloucester railway station to meet what looked like a gigantic Christmas tree, as Alex emerged from the carriage festooned with every accoutrement that the RAF had ever dreamed up, from kit bag to drinking mug. What with that and the undesired posting itself, it was a bleak watery smile that answered my genial greeting. He dumped his kit bag on the platform, pointed and said, "*You* did this to me, you did. What in God's name gives you the power?" I meekly pointed to my Leading Aircraftman badge and said, "You think this gives me power? Really, Alex, what an imagination." He was still grumbling as I bundled him into a taxi. I then explained the whole situation and assured him there would be little change in his various professional assignments. I introduced him to Flight Lt. Eldred the following day and they got on splendidly together; thereafter for reasons best known to himself, he always referred to Eldred as the "Mother Superior."

The first edition of "Off the Record" was a complete sellout and a great success, proving that, as I had insisted, anything paid for is appreciated more than if it comes free.

So life continued happily enough; I appeared with the RAF Choral Society in the Messiah in Gloucester Methodist Church. I also teamed up again with Harry Engleman, who was still stationed in Blackpool, and we did some more recordings of "Services Calling" for the BBC. One big problem on my mind, however, was the appalling dressing room accommodation at the concert hall, which was nothing more than a rope across the room with blankets draped over it, so I decided to go and see the group captain to ask that something be done about it. I knocked on the door and entered on his command. There he sat at a great desk like a high altar, stacked so high by shoals of highly confidential documents and various colored telephones that he was virtually out of sight. I rapidly went into an explanation of the problem and found myself saying such things as, "They are an absolute disgrace for anybody, let alone star artists who come here." He wriggled in his chair a bit and then said he would get on to the nearby maintenance unit and get them to construct proper facilities. "I am going to London," I said, "to do some recordings for the BBC. I shall be returning next Wednesday morning. I know you are an extremely busy man but I don't want to find when I get back that you have done nothing about it." To my utter amazement this high ranking officer with four "thick-uns" on his sleeve jumped up from his chair, saluted me and said, "I will see that it is done, Sir." My evident confusion was clearly too obvious for the group captain to miss, and I felt that he was drawing some satisfaction from my loss of confidence as I stammered, "Thank you very much," and stumbled out of the office.

Although everything was running smoothly and the dressing rooms were done, with the pressures of running the shows, including the difficult rehearsals, and the other odd engagements that came my way, I was feeling the strain, and perhaps I should have taken more care of myself. I was on my way to London to a recording session and afterward I had arranged to meet Frank Eldred at the theatrical costumiers. I was feeling as though a bad cold was just around the corner, and when we had finished Frank Eldred insisted that we went to a pub, as he said that by the look of me, I needed a double whisky. I gladly accepted it and for a time it gave me a certain amount of relief, but I soon began to feel bad again, and so headed for home and straight to bed. Never in my wildest dreams could I have imagined that my drink with Eldred was to be my last link with the Royal Air Force.

*M*orning dawned and I struggled into wakefulness from a troubled sleep. I felt worse than before, my throat painful and breathing a labor of frightening proportions. My mother, greatly alarmed, sent for our family doctor, whose countenance after examination gave little cause for optimism. He left hurriedly after taking a swab from my throat and an hour later an ambulance arrived and I was being rushed to the fever hospital. I was soon ensconced in a bed where, in spite of the wretchedness that had engulfed me, I lay fretting and worrying over the next production, which was too important to be jeopardized by any nonsense such as being ill.

When the matron and a senior doctor put in an appearance I immediately made it clear to them that I was far too busy to be ill and that I must be on my way as soon as possible. Obviously well indoctrinated into the idiotic remarks of patients, they managed a wintry smile and explained that I had diphtheria. I remember replying quite seriously, "Thank goodness for that, it's only a kid's complaint isn't it? So if you give me the right pills or injections I'll be back in Gloucester in time to organize the show next week."

The matron responded like a long-suffering mother chastising her child, "Really young man, your show will have to get on without you. The very minimum time you will spend with us is six weeks." I gazed at her in disbelief and repeated, "Six weeks?" "Yes," she said, "at least," and furiously patting my pillows added, "You're the star of this show and we are the audience, so muck in, do as you're told and we'll all give you a round of applause when you walk out of the door." I lay back and contemplated with horror the six-week sentence that had so firmly been passed on me.

By the time I had passed the crisis and been saved from slowly choking to death I gradually became so weak that I couldn't summon enough strength to squeeze the toothpaste from a tube. Apparently in extremely bad cases of diphtheria, *all* of the muscles of the body are savagely attacked and a form of paralysis sets in. Thus, it was that although at first I was so glad to be alive that nothing else worried me, then the specter of a life in which show business no longer played a part began to occupy my mind every waking moment. As I looked at my useless fingers, which had lost all their dexterity, I could not believe that I would ever again be capable of playing the piano. And when, nearly six months after entering the hospital, I finally returned home I felt that my career was at an end and life as I would wish to live it was also ended.

I started all over again, just as if I were back in Miss Stein's School. Hour after hour I sat at the piano, practicing scales, arpeggios, and studies. At times I would despair and begin to consider what other forms of livelihood I could take up. Only those who have experienced it can understand the frustration of trying to use fingers that are sloppy and weak and have very little feeling in them. Thankfully, the encouragement I received as a child from those about me when I first sat at a piano was repeated now and, together with my own dogged determination, finally, carried me through. It wasn't until the wonderful moment when I began playing sufficiently well again that I was able to consider accepting a professional engagement.

In spite of all I had gone through, I was still in the RAF and officially just on convalescent leave, and I was well aware that at any time I might be sent for to rejoin my unit. However, in view of my undeniably poor state of health, plus the fact that the war was obviously moving toward its close, I felt that there was a fair chance I might not be recalled and that I ought, therefore, to look to the future.

When playing for Elsie Carlisle at the BBC Studios in Bangor, I had frequently met Charles Shadwell, conductor of the famous BBC Variety Orchestra. We had got on well together and he had asked me to get in touch with him when I left the RAF. Although still technically in the service, I was convinced that *this* was the moment, so I rang him up. His response was most encouraging and he put me in touch with the orchestral manager, Gwen Potter, who arranged an audition as a matter of urgency, not because they were so anxious to have *me* but because they were desperately in need of a pianist.

My audition took place at the BBC's Aeolian Hall and was in two parts. I had to demonstrate my ability to play both classical and popular type music and to prove my ability to sight read. There were quite a number of other applicants for the position and although I believed I had done reasonably well, I still had not recovered in full the confidence I had lost during my illness, and so I felt I had little chance. I cannot describe the utter joy that I felt when a few days later I was informed that I had, in fact, been accepted—subject to a month's trial. It put me right back on my feet and from then on I never looked back. It was the boost to my morale that I had so desperately needed. I have always been grateful that I was judged on my merits alone and not condemned on medical grounds. I was still obliged to walk with the aid of a stick and I had feared that this might have influenced Shadwell.

My luck had indeed turned, because shortly after the audition I was summoned to attend a medical board, which concluded that although fit enough to continue service in the RAF, I could have my medical discharge if I were to sign a document exonerating the RAF from any responsibility for my illness, incapacity, and general loss occasioned by it. Needless to say I readily signed on the dotted line! Thus on June 25, 1945, I became a full-fledged civilian again!

The war had ended about six weeks previously, bringing happiness and relief noisily expressed by millions, although I myself still did not feel fit enough to display my feelings in an active way.

I have never been a pushy sort of fellow, preferring rather to rely on my talent itself to bring success. To be accepted by Charles Shadwell as a member of the BBC Variety Orchestra was a very encouraging start. Working for the orchestra was quite a challenge and the degree of perfection that was demanded was such that only one rehearsal of each piece was allowed: every member of the orchestra just had to have the considerable expertise necessary or they would not have survived. In spite of this I enjoyed every minute of it. The remuneration £27 ($135.00) a week wasn't too bad for those days and the hours were quite reasonable, averaging thirty a week spread over five or six days. Many of the programs, such as "ITMA," went out live either from the Paris Cinema in Regent Street or the Criterion. Other famous shows that I took part in included "Music Hall," "Navy Mixture," and "Monday Night at Eight." There was also a weekly orchestral concert where I was featured in special arrangements for the piano.

It was about this time that I decided to get married; I had known Leila O'Dwyer since 1939 and with the war now behind us we made a trip to Caxton Hall in 1945 and then set up home in a furnished flat in Ealing. As a married man, who because of his position in show business needed to keep up a certain standard of living, I now found my BBC remuneration inadequate for the purpose. I decided to remedy this by looking around for an additional job. I was lucky enough to get a regular engagement at the Dorchester Hotel in Park Lane, where for six evenings a week I would play the piano for half an hour, starting at 10:00 p.m. This, plus the odd occasion when I would deputize for the pianist for the whole evening, brought me in an additional £25 ($125.00) per week. It was a great help and compared very favorably indeed with the wage I was receiving from the BBC. The contract I had with them did, of course, guarantee that they had first call on my services at all times but I was, nevertheless able to keep the Dorchester going and even do the odd fifteen minutes solo broadcast featuring a star vocalist for the BBC. This program went out either as "Piano Playtime" or "Star Time."

It was about this time that I met up with the other Eric Barker. He and his wife, Pearl Hackney, were doing regular broadcasts and the occasion arose when I was involved in one of them. We were talking together when Pearl quite gratuitously referred to the extraordinary "cock up" that had occurred during the early part of the war. She disclosed the fact that her husband had received call-up papers together with travel warrants to join the RAF. She had written back to explain that it would be difficult for him to comply as he was already serving in the Royal Navy. This explanation had no effect whatsoever because a duplicate set of papers arrived a few weeks later. She again returned them and again explained. When a third set arrived, she simply threw them in the fire and did the same when yet a fourth lot turned up. The outcome of all this was the embarrassing incident I suffered.

Shortly after this conversation I was sitting in the BBC canteen with singer Anne Shelton and producer Joy Russell-Smith and I told them the story of the call-up fiasco and Joy immediately said that I should regard the incident as an indication of the problems that can arise when two people in show business share an identical name and that I should remedy the matter immediately by choosing a different one. After some further discussion, Joy came up with a compromise that I immediately found acceptable. "Don't change your name," she said, "just drop the surname. Eric James runs easily off the tongue and will look good on a poster or play bill." So from that moment on, the second Eric Barker departed. The BBC was very pleased, because they had experienced a lot of difficulty when trying to deliver fan mail to the correct Eric Barker. Charlie Shadwell, in his usual kind and considerate way, lost no time in getting my new name across to the public.

I cannot touch upon the story of my stay with the BBC without referring to some of the artists whom I accompanied: Maggie Teyte had a simply glorious voice. Alfredo Campoli was a fine violinist for whom I played; among the pieces that we did together was the very demanding "Flight of the Bumble Bee." I played for Gracie Fields just once, in the unusual venue of the Radio Exhibition at Earls Court; she was a real trouper and a joy to be with. My involvement with the extremely popular program "In Town Tonight" resulted in my meeting and accompanying scores of celebrities. The show went out live every Saturday at 7:00 p.m. and rehearsals were seldom possible because some of the personalities would literally walk into the studio just a few minutes before we were on the air. I cannot mention everybody but among the guests I met and was pleased to play for were Joan Hammond, Lana Turner, Harry Secombe, Carole Carr, Vera Lynn, and Tony Martin.

Another lovely artist for whom I played was Ann Blyth, who had just arrived in London after making a film with Mario Lanza. She must have been pleased with my efforts because a few days later I was asked to accompany her at a special ball being held at Grosvenor House for an engagement party at which Prince Philip and Princess Elizabeth were guests of honor. Promptly at 11:00 p.m. a grand piano was pushed on to the floor of the Great Room and there in front of a thousand guests we did our cabaret spot; among the numbers was "Embraceable You," which created quite a stir because Ann sang it directly and solely to Prince Philip. As a result of this most successful date I was given a very excellent fee—taken out by Ann to dinner at the Wardroom on Curzon Street and afterward invited to her suite at the Dorchester for a drink and to meet her aunt and uncle who had accompanied her from the United States.

In 1947, after a couple of years with the orchestra, Charles Shadwell confided that he felt he had stayed with the BBC long enough and it was high time he took advantage of his immense popularity with the public to leave the "BEEB" and tour the British Isles with his own orchestra. He asked how I felt about following his example and coming with him in the capacity of pianist/manager, as he felt that my experience in both capacities would make me ideal for the job.

Our first task was to form the orchestra itself and this meant many hours auditioning musicians. We rehearsed like blazes until we felt confident enough to let the agent, Leslie McDonnell of Fosters Agency, see a complete run through.

He liked it immensely and in a very short time he had negotiated a long tour of all the principal theaters in the British Isles. He also pulled off the major achievement of booking us for the Moss Empire Circuit. It was universally recognized as the hallmark of one's box-office pulling power to be accepted by the Moss Empire. What is more, in virtually every theater, we were given the entire second half of the program. It was, however, a tough assignment and extremely exhausting. On one occasion we were booked by impresario Harold Fielding to give twenty-one concerts in twenty-one days in January, ranging in venue from Southend-on-Sea to Aberdeen in the extreme north of Scotland. It was literally like being in a circus; finish a show late at night, up at the crack of dawn and away to another town and another concert hall, only to repeat the whole thing over and over again.

On another occasion, also during the winter, we were appearing at the Shepherds Bush Empire (now used exclusively by the BBC). Charles invited me to join him for a quick visit to a friend who lived in nearby Notting Hill Gate. He suggested doing it after the first house, as he felt that would give us time enough. Clad in my old RAF boots, not a pretty sight with the upper lace holes undone, but essential in order to negotiate the snow and slush to where the car was parked, we set off to enjoy this brief relaxation. Needless to say we stopped longer than we should have and by the time we got back to the theater, there was only ten minutes before "curtain up." To make matters worse, a group of close friends of Charles were waiting at the stage door for his arrival.

Being too engrossed with the needs of getting himself ready for a performance, he asked me to deal with them and fix them up with complimentary seats. I did this and was hurrying back stage when I was horrified to hear the voice of the emcee coming over the public address system actually introducing us. I threw off my overcoat and ran to the piano, arriving just before the house lights were lowered and the curtain swung back, revealing a grand piano bathed in the spotlight, with myself immaculate in white tie and tails, well groomed, if a little out of breath. I struck the first chords of Grieg's Piano Concerto in A Minor, a very dramatic moment that would normally have thrilled and hushed the audience into concentrated silence, but on this occasion there was a spontaneous peal of laughter from both audience and orchestra alike. I was mystified and astonished until I saw Charles pointing to my feet, on which still resided my huge, dirty RAF boots! There was absolutely nothing I could do about it. I just had to keep playing, but those forty-five minutes aged me considerably.

The tour was a complete success and we did enormous business at every theater at which we appeared. We approached the second tour with equal enthusiasm, but after a few months of diminished box office returns we were losing money every week and the sad decision was made to disband the show. Charles and I remained friends for many years thereafter. He continued to appear at various venues and was always well received, while I went into partnership with George Myddleton, famous resident pianist with the "Workers Playtime" BBC program, to form a new piano duo, and we toured theaters and concert halls all over the country. The BBC also took a liking to our work and we did scores of broadcasts including several radio series. We traveled together playing to good and not so good houses, but on the whole we were received very well and made a reasonable living.

Early in 1950 the ill health of his wife forced George to terminate our partnership. He was desperately unhappy to break up such a popular and successful act but he quite rightly put the need to look after his wife before everything else. This left me on my own but with the same need to earn my living, so I decided to continue as a solo entertainer. Unfortunately things weren't made any easier by the fact that theaters were beginning to disappear and even large cinemas that sometimes took on a live act were becoming bingo halls. However, I still managed to get quite a few engagements, one of which was on a variety bill at the Brixton Empress Theatre.

In one part of my act I used to play the Can Can section from

"Orpheus in the Underworld," and I would feature the trombone in the orchestra. While this instrument was blasting away at the famous melody I would pull up my right trouser leg displaying a large red garter with a bright diamentè piece of jewelry attached. At the appropriate bars of music I would vigorously kick up my leg in time to it, the drummer punctuating each kick with a loud crash on the cymbals. After the inevitable laugh had died away I would drop the trouser leg and carry on playing normally. On this particular night after just one kick, the folding chair on which I was seated collapsed completely and I fell flat on my back on the floor. The audience and pit orchestra thought it hilarious, which was more than I did. However, I managed to put on a brave face and I announced that as I broke a seat at every performance the management had decided to increase the price of admission—mock groans from all sides!

I should imagine that there is not a person in show business who could not relate tales of unrehearsed incidents but I must say that I seem to have had more than my fair share. Following hard on the fiasco just described came another incident that occurred when I accompanied comediennes Gert and Daisy (Elsie and Doris Waters), at a concert at the Winter Gardens, Eastbourne. I was completely dressed and ready to go on when I discovered that from the two pairs of patent leather shoes that I had at home, I had brought both of the left ones. I had no alternative but to put them on. They looked quite ridiculous to anyone near enough to see them properly but I might have got away with it as far as the audience was concerned had not Elsie, out of sheer devilment, in introducing me as their accompanist, added that they were very proud to have me as I was the only pianist in world with two left feet! I could cheerfully have strangled her. Actually I loved them both dearly and always enjoyed the occasions when I appeared with them.

Of all the happy times we had together there cannot have been any more outstanding than when many years later we were invited to a private party given by the Duke and Duchess of Norfolk at Arundel Castle. Of course we had to "sing for our supper" and we duly gave a short performance. It must have gone down well because when supper was announced His Grace invited us to sit at his table. I was privileged to be placed next to him and it gave me the opportunity to congratulate him on his brilliant organization of the

Myself at the piano, aged thirteen. (Author's collection)

A formal portrait, aged twenty. (Author's collection)

At the time of my first work with Chaplin. (Author's collection)

Chaplin playing around during the music recording of *A King in New York,* 1956. (Roy Export Company Establishment)

"A Thousand Windows Smile at Me," inscribed to me by Chaplin in 1956. (Author's collection)

The Manoir de Ban,
Chaplin's home in
Corsier, near Vevey,
Switzerland.
(Jeffrey Vance
collection)

Charlie and Oona
on the terrace of the
Manoir, 1958.
(Author's
collection)

This 1958
snapshot of Oona
and me was taken
by Charlie.
(Author's
collection)

This photograph, taken by Oona, was Charlie's favorite picture of himself.
(Author's collection)

To Eric — the best ever musically —
Charlie Chaplin

Charlie and I during the music recording of A *Countess from Hong Kong* at the Anvil Studios, Denham, 1966. (Author's collection)

Charlie conferring with me during the music recording of *A Countess from Hong Kong*. Bill Williamson is in the foreground. (Author's collection)

Charlie playing an imaginary flute during the music recording of
A Countess from Hong Kong. (Author's collection)

Charlie holding the conductor's baton during the music recording
of *A Countess from Hong Kong.* (Author's collection)

With Oona and Charlie at the time of the music recording of *A Countess from Hong Kong.* (Author's collection)

The Chaplin family, photographed in 1968. The children from left are: Josephine, Jane (sitting), Michael, Geraldine, Christopher (sitting in front of Geraldine), Eugene, Victoria, and Annette (sitting in front of Vicky). Charlie and Oona celebrated their twenty-fifth wedding anniversary that year. (Roy Export Company Establishment)

Charlie and I outside the Manoir after Josephine Chaplin's wedding
in June 1969. (Author's collection)

Charlie and Oona photographed in the salon of the Manoir in 1971.
(Author's collection)

Ken Cameron (the managing director of Anvil Studios) and his brother James
Cameron with Charlie, Rachel Ford, Oona, and me outside the
Land of Liberty pub, circa 1973. (Author's collection)

Charlie and I look at the new road extension to Montreux, which crossed one
corner of the Manoir, circa 1974. (Author's collection)

Charlie's inscription in my copy of his 1974 book
My Life in Pictures. (Roy Export Company Establishment)

Charlie and I take a break on the terrace of the Manoir in 1976.
(Author's collection)

The last formal portrait of Charlie, taken on his birthday in April 1977.
Oona used this photograph as the family Christmas card that year.
(Roy Export Company Establishment)

With my wife and partner, Phyllis O'Reilly, around the time of our first
"A Tribute to Charlie Chaplin." (Author's collection)

Charles Chaplin in costume and make-up as "The Little Tramp," circa 1916.
(Roy Export Company Establishment)

recent funeral of Winston Churchill, a ceremony for which he, as the Earl Marshall of England, was responsible. He disclosed that originally there had been six members of Churchill's funeral committee, but when the time came, only he and one other were still alive, which made the task even more arduous. He went on to say that when he finally got back to Arundel after it was all over he was so exhausted that he almost crawled through the door to be greeted by his wife, Lavinia, who said, "Go and have a hot bath, dear, put on your dressing gown, then come down, have a cup of tea and see yourself on television." I thought that indicated a wonderful, domesticated homely side to the life of such an exalted person as the Earl Marshall of England and Premier Duke of Great Britain.

It was in 1950 that I began a long association with the Combined Services Entertainment (CSE). This, a successor to the famous war time ENSA, was created in order to serve the needs of the British troops still deployed in stations all over the world. When Col. George Brightwell of the War Office invited me to join a small company of artists to tour overseas, I readily accepted. Our first assignment was in Germany. The tour was extremely successful and indeed we were asked to repeat it.

Early in 1952 I was asked by the BBC and CSE to do a six-week tour of the Middle East in a radio series starring Frankie Howerd, which was to be recorded at some venues and subsequently broadcast in the British Isles. The scripts were to be written by Eric Sykes, who would be a member of the company. He went out of his way to be as completely "up to the minute" and as topical as possible, taking into consideration the location in the Middle East and type of serviceman audience that we would be entertaining. The series was produced by Roy Speir; in addition we had a BBC engineer to deal with the recordings.

Our first stop was Cyprus where for a week we provided entertainment at the largest troop camps. Our last show was at Nicosia and afterward we were entertained in the Officers Mess. Unfortunately, I was latched onto by a very patronizing junior officer, and in order to extricate myself and so be free to circulate, I decided to carry out my old ploy of "double talk," i.e., the use of nonsensical words that are made to sound as if they are real ones. I therefore asked the officer if, in his opinion, "the use of the napid mutes in the ristans of the present day orchestras should be encouraged."

He immediately said, "Oh yes, I think so," and equally quickly I asked, "In what proportions?" His face fell, he mumbled "Ah," then, looking at his watch, said, "My God, is that the time? I was due on duty ten minutes ago; nice talking to you"—and he was gone! What I did not realize was that my conversation had been overheard by our engineer, who must have thought that my gobble-de-gook seemed very poor stuff. "What an over joy to meet to meet you, Eric," he said. "We must fallow up ourselves on every occasion with a ready-mix blasto of chosen well conversaitch." His name was Stanley Unwin and he became famous for this comedic delivery. We became very close friends and we had some good laughs wherever we went. By the way, the incident just described occurred the evening before we were due to fly from Nicosia to Fayad in Egypt. Our specially chartered plane was due to take off at 10:00 a.m. but to us, who had worked so hard and then been entertained so generously, 10:00 a.m. seemed the middle of the night. Feeling as frail as we did, we prevailed upon Stanley Unwin to phone the airport and explain in his own inimitable way that following the indisposition of Frankie Howerd we had been held up and could they hold the plane until noon. Stan had introduced himself to the officer in charge of flights as a senior medical officer and his detailed medical double talk, which he used to explain Frankie's condition, was the most fantastic load of "cobblers" that has ever been my good fortune to listen to. The airport controller was of course completely lost by it all but expressed great sympathy and readily agreed to the two-hour delay.

Our travels took us all over the canal zone and one of the first shows we did there was on Lord Louis Mountbatten's flagship *HMS Glasgow*. The piano I was using was an excellent upright Bechstein that had been obtained, after great difficulty, by the stage manager of the CSE. It was very seldom that I was ever lucky enough to get a piano other than the type that was teetering on the edge of the scrap heap. Incidentally, *HMS Glasgow* was anchored at Port Said and we were accommodated at the Eastern Exchange Hotel, from where we were taken the following morning to the army camp at El Ballah. We set off at about 10:00 a.m. and our stage manager Mr. Mazzola decided to stop off at the *Glasgow* en route, just to make certain that our highly valued Bechstein had been successfully reloaded on to our three-tonner.

Upon our arrival, Mr. Mazzola jumped out and cheerily called to an officer, "Just called back to check that you've off-loaded our piano OK. Where is it?" The officer, who we now noticed, had a face of one who had just seen the ghost of Nelson, uttered not a word but pointed to a spot further down the quay. We all turned and looked toward a pile of matchwood from which protruded strands of wire and the odd piece of ivory. We all walked toward it and stood in a silent, tight-lipped circle, not believing what we were looking at. The duty officer hurried over to us, literally wringing his hands. "I'm so frightfully sorry but we have had, as you can see, a little accident." I could only exclaim, "Mother of Mary, how little is little." Mazzola, his face now twitching with suppressed anger, asked how it happened and when told that the ropes hadn't been secured properly, he retorted with considerable feeling, "I thought you bloody sailors had to learn how to tie knots." I ruefully picked up a piano key and said, "I know my playing has on occasions brought the house down but this is ridiculous."

We enjoyed our six-week tour immensely and it had been successful wherever we went; alas when the recorded concerts were put over the air by the BBC, the reaction from the public was very disappointing. It was particularly sad for Eric Sykes, who had done a marvelous job of writing the scripts, sometimes under great difficulties. However, he, like the rest of us, took solace in the fact that at least the servicemen enjoyed them.

My next tour was far less exotic though still enjoyable and interesting. My wife and I were living at Gerrards Cross with her brother-in-law, a retired Harley Street dental surgeon. Virtually all of our furniture, apart from the Bluthner Grand piano, was in storage and the future was looking a little uncertain, when I received a phone call from the War Office. Col. George Brightwell asked if I would do a three-week tour of British camps in Austria with Bill Johnson, who had starred on stage in "Annie Get Your Gun." I accepted like a shot; a special messenger arrived and dealt with all the documentation at a speed that only the War Office could have conjured up, and within forty-eight hours I was landing in Vienna. An officer was there to meet me; he was in a great state of agitation and said that we had not a minute to waste as we just had to get to the railway station in order to catch the 2:30 p.m. train to Klagenfurt.

I felt as if my feet were not touching the ground as he virtually dragged me at high speed through passport and custom control, sweeping those august institutions aside with authoritative disdain. A jeep was waiting outside with its engine already running over. We threw ourselves in and the driver sped off like a bat out of hell; one moment I had been getting up from my seat in the plane, and the next moment I was in a speeding jeep in the heart of Vienna. It was really all too much and the feeling that it was all a nightmare increased when the vehicle began to splutter violently before coming to a complete standstill; I did not need to understand German to get the gist from the Austrian driver that we were out of petrol. Surely, I thought, this must be the end of the fantasy.

However, my officer escort, without a moment's hesitation, rushed from the jeep to the electric tramway, where, to my astonishment he stopped a tram that was coming along and instructed the driver to drive us both to the railway station as fast as he could go, nonstop. So off we went, standing with the driver and me holding on for dear life as the vehicle swayed violently under its unaccustomed speed. Would-be passengers holding out their arms at tram stops and passengers already in the tram, continually ringing the bell to get off, were all ignored, as the tram driver, with obvious pleasure at his newfound power, raced unerringly over the rails toward those other rails at the station, at which we arrived in five minutes flat.

I raced with my luggage to platform one while the officer sped to the Railway Transport Office office to collect my ticket. Gasping for breath I dragged myself up the three steps of the nearest carriage and as I reached the top, the train started to pull out with the officer racing alongside just in time to throw the ticket and some Austrian money into the open door. They fell on to the floor where I had myself slumped with exhaustion, and remained there for some minutes until I found the strength to retrieve them, pick myself up, and find a seat in the nearest compartment. An hour later I was tucking into some sausages and coffee brought round to the compartment by a steward and I was at last able to draw breath and prepare for what I hoped would be a more peaceful arrival at Klagenfurt.

I was met on arrival by Dr. Inge Morze, the British Occupation Army of the Rhine entertainment representative, who lost no time in getting me to the Moser Hotel, where I was to stay. Bill Johnson was already there but had no music with him, having just flown in from Rome where he had been making a film. We sat down to a meal together to discuss the routine for our two-man shows. We later found an upright piano in the hotel so we were able to get in a rehearsal before doing our first concert next evening at an army barracks. We put on a show lasting just under two hours and it was a tremendous success, so we decided to stick to that format for the rest of the tour. After a show in Herman Goering's favorite spot, Graz, we were sitting in our hotel feeling rather despondent because of the uncertainty of being able to get through to our next venue—Vienna. At the time of this tour, Austria was still under the joint occupation of the British, American, French, and Russian troops, who each policed it for one month, in rotation. We were there during the turn of the Russians, who, alone of the four powers, made life difficult during their term of duty. The special gray card travel permit was given to me without difficulty, but they refused to give one to Bill because he was an American.

We were discussing this somewhat vehemently and, unbeknown to us, our comments were heard by Capt. Hughes, aide-de-camp to the British ambassador, Sir Harold Caccia. The following morning, to our joy and astonishment, he rang up to explain that having heard us, he took the liberty of mentioning the matter to Sir Harold, who had promptly instructed him to offer us a lift in his private plane, thus avoiding the problem of the gray card as we would not be travelling through the Semmering Pass for which the gray card was needed. We were given forty-five minutes to get to the airport, but we were there in thirty! The ambassador greeted us warmly and ushered us into the eight-seat Rapide, which took off immediately. In less than an hour we were on the tarmac of the military airport at Vienna. A Rolls Royce was awaiting the ambassador's arrival and in minutes we were driving through a city that meant so much to me as a musician.

We had filled in the time of the flight telling Sir Harold all about our activities and he obviously wanted to continue to help us. When we arrived at the embassy he and his aide disembarked, and then he instructed the driver to take us to the Park Hotel, where we were to stay. We both agreed that our transport was a marked improvement to the three-ton truck we were travelling in the previous day.

Naturally, we felt more than pleased that our conversation had been overheard way back in Graz, but we had to return to the real world and that meant the first of our concerts in Vienna would be the same evening. I was stunned, therefore, when during a break offstage, I was called to the telephone where a voice at the other end introduced herself as Lady Caccia. She proceeded to apologize for the fact that Sir Harold had not invited us to stay at the embassy. "I was furious with my husband when he told me he had left you at the Park Hotel," she said. She went on to invite the pair of us to a party at the embassy that evening that was being given in honor of some general who was leaving Vienna the following day. It would have been churlish to refuse such an invitation!

The minute I had finished the National Anthem at the close of our concert that evening, Bill and I, clad in our stage evening dress suits, were on our way to the embassy. We were charmingly received and introduced rapidly to many of the other guests before sitting down to a wonderful meal that included caviar, smoked salmon and a most excellent champagne. After such an outstanding repast we felt that the least we could do was to offer to entertain our host, hostess, and fellow guests. The suggestion being enthusiastically received, I took my place at the Steinway grand piano and for the next half hour we regaled the assembled company with numbers from the various musical comedies in which Bill had starred. We kept it to the half hour because experience had taught us both that it is always best to leave when one is winning. It was about 3:00 a.m. when Sir Harold and Lady Caccia accompanied us down the long winding marble staircase to say our farewells and thanks in the hallway of the embassy. As we shook hands Sir Harold said, "I hope you won't think me presumptuous but I thought if your had some spare time tomorrow you might be able to find a use for an embassy car that I will be happy to place at your disposal." It was a most generous offer and a wonderful end to a very enjoyable evening.

The following morning we were down at 9:30 a.m. as arranged and there, by the hotel entrance, we found a Humber Limousine with liveried chauffeur awaiting us. Feeling highly elated we told him to simply spend the day taking us to everything worth seeing. He did just that and by the time we had finished we were suffering from cultural indigestion. We were so tired that it took a great deal of effort to do our concert the next evening. However, somehow we still found the strength to do the show, have a meal at the famous restaurant, on the low ceiling of which hundreds of famous people have left their autographs, and attend a performance of *La Boheme* at the State Opera House. So ended a memorable visit to Vienna, made possible thanks to the extraordinary kindness and consideration of the man who so ably represented Great Britain's interests with the support of his charming wife.

The following day we started our journey south, continuing our series of concerts and enjoying the beautiful mountains and lakes.

Our final concert in Trieste was as successful as all the rest, and Bill included songs he had made his own, such as "They Say That Falling in Love Is Wonderful," "So in Love," and "The Girl that I Marry." It was a joy to be with him and it came as a great shock when his death at the age of forty-four was announced only two years later.

However, a very interesting and happy engagement was to follow when I was invited by the War Office Entertainment Department to join a concert party for a tour of Asia to be headed by Elizabeth "Liz" Webb, who had just completed a long run of "Bless the Bride" in London's West End. The other artists in the party were Eddie Leslie (a comedian who was currently working with Norman Wisdom), Joan Seton (an attractive soubrette), and Harold Childs (versatile tap-dancer).

In those days long distance travel was quite an ordeal; we left Heathrow on a Tuesday evening arriving in Hong Kong late Saturday afternoon. The CSE representative was awaiting us and we were soon installed in the very beautiful colonial-style Peninsula Hotel. Here we were allocated really nice suites, which we much appreciated, but which I was sure bore no resemblance to the type of accommodation that we would be allocated elsewhere. As I remarked to Liz, who was so pleased with such a high standard, "Make the most of it dear, we are starting at the top and we will undoubtedly work our way down." Before leaving Hong Kong, I went to see Curtis Hindson, who was the director general of the Hong Kong Broadcasting Corp. I told him that Liz Webb and I would be back in the colony in six-weeks' time and would he be interested in engaging us to do a number of fifteen-minute piano and voice recordings. He was delighted with the idea and asked us to come to the studios as soon as we arrived back.

Shortly after this interview our Argonaut was "chugging" its way over the two thousand miles to Tokyo where on arrival we were taken to the officers Transit Camp at Ebisu barracks. What with the marked contrast to the Peninsula Hotel, the drizzling rain, and the unfavorable first impression of Tokyo, we felt somewhat deflated. Later I took a trip by subway to the center of Tokyo and made my way to the Ginza. I saw very little that has remained as a lasting impression but I do recall the odd sight of people wearing facemasks, both as a protection for others when the wearer has a cold and as a filter against the terrible exhaust fumes in the streets. It was a good idea but it did give the impression that Tokyo was given over to a gigantic surgeon's convention!

Leaving Japan, we continued on to our ultimate destination: Korea. We landed at Pusan and were again given accommodations at a nearby barracks.

Pusan was a dreadful place and the troops we met described it as the "arsehole" of the world; we found no reason to disagree with such an apt description! We were more than glad when it was time to leave and go north to Seoul, a city that had changed hands three times in eighteen months and was consequently in a terrible state, with few houses still standing. The following day we moved nearer to the front line but thankfully were quartered three miles behind the front line safely in the rear with the 57th Company of the Royal Army Service Corps. Major Bill Paterson, the commanding officer, greeted us most affably and personally conducted us to our "hoochies," small dwellings of mud and lathes construction that were basic to say the least. The major had gallantly given up his own hoochie to Liz and Joan, where he had coconut matting put on the duckboard floor and had provided two iron beds, a couple of chairs and a table, while he himself slept in the back of a three-ton truck. He was obviously startled when Liz, who was writing a letter to her mother, suddenly looked up and asked, "How to you spell squalor?" Actually, he and everybody laughed but she was always known thereafter as "Miss Squalor." Uncle Bill, as Major Paterson was referred to by his troops, really did his best to make us feel at home and wanted, and his personality and many kindnesses enabled us to put up with the privations we were experiencing.

Subsequently we were taken by Col. Carne to see the area where the glorious Gloucesters made their famous stand. After hearing and seeing all we could, including a view of the distant territory occupied by the enemy across the Imjin River, we returned to our camp. It was there a few days later that we received a signal from Hong Kong offering us six fifteen-minute recorded broadcasts at $200 Hong Kong per program; Liz and I were delighted. We agreed to split the money and immediately sent a signal of acceptance.

After six weeks, our tour of Korea was over. We were flown back to Tokyo in an American "Globemaster" and from there another plane took us on to Hong Kong.

We contacted Mr. Hindson as soon as we arrived back in Hong Kong and we made recording arrangements for 10:00 a.m. the next day. By 1:20 p.m. Liz and I completed our task to the satisfaction of everyone and departed to our hotel, both of us $600 richer. The following day I flew back to England leaving the others to return in a more leisurely fashion.

In 1955 I was engaged for a twenty-four-week summer season at the Gaiety Theatre in Ayr, Scotland. The name of the show was "Gaiety Whirl" and, although the cast was changed, it went under the same name year after year and had in fact become an institution with the Scots. Because of this, we played to a full house during the entire run of the show. It was a very happy company and there was also an added bonus in the shape of my sister-in-law, Veronica. She had married Freddy, eldest son of Sir Charles Dunlop, whose large mansion "Doonside" was situated on the outskirts of the town. My wife and I had rented a nearby bungalow for the season and she was able to spend most of her time with her sister at the mansion, while I was privileged to go salmon fishing in the River Doon, which ran through the estate. It was peaceful and very pleasant but I never succeeded in landing a single fish. I was, however, able to experience a little of what it's like to be one of the landed gentry.

Part Two

Life with Charlie Chaplin

CHAPTER 1

$\mathcal{O}$n 1956 I formed a partnership with my old friend the superb organist Robinson Cleaver. We did this in the hope that it would provide a regular income and so help out during the periods when engagements were few and far between. We gave our agency the grandiose title of Sound Music Publishing Co., a name that was a good deal more imposing than the small room we rented on Denmark Street. In a way it was a bit of a cheek on our part to set ourselves up in Tin Pan Alley, as the street was known, because it already housed music agencies in every nook and cranny. On the other hand, as this was the center of the British music world, it did seem reasonable that we could hope to do business, even if only because interested parties lost their way and walked through our door in error!

Although money did trickle in we were doomed to failure because we could not afford to create a really commercially viable catalog of music. We needed at least a hundred really first class numbers but we hadn't got them; it was as simple as that. We struggled on for two years and then sold out to Peter Maurice Music Co. for a few hundred pounds. It was a pity, but I never regret doing it. I learned a very great deal and enjoyed the experience of once again being part of that great mecca of music. Apart from this it was thanks to our venture that I was to embark on the most interesting period of my life.

The spring weather of 1956 was extremely good. Sitting in the office one day with nothing particular happening I thought that perhaps a quick stroll around the block in the brilliant sunshine might freshen me up and thus help me to deal with the flood of business that hopefully might lie ahead! As joint owner of the concern I naturally kept my nose to the grindstone, but I thought that ten minutes in the sun was hardly likely to drastically affect our overall situation. I moved toward the door and had just begun to open it when the phone rang. I turned, picked up the receiver, and heard the voice of Jimmy Phillips, managing director of Peter Maurice Music Co., speaking from his office next door. He was ringing to tell me that some work was available at Shepperton Film Studios and would I be interested. As it is always policy never to say "yes" to something immediately, but to "hum and ha" a bit as if one is trying to work to in to a packed engagement book, I just crackled some papers and "tumpty tummed" a bit, when Jimmy casually added that the job was for Charlie Chaplin and involved post synchronization. I blinked, gulped, and then as nonchalantly as I could, agreed to go down to the studios the following morning. Within minutes a top line copy of the music was delivered to me by hand. Later on Jimmy told me that had I not answered the phone he would have had to ask elsewhere, as it was too urgent to hold. As the call was destined to change the whole pattern of my life for the next twenty years, I shudder at the thought that I might have been strolling in the sun and missed it.

The film in which this music was to be used was *A King in New York*, a short sequence of which depicted an actor playing a piano to which had been fitted a dummy keyboard. My job was to provide the missing sound, matching it to the movements and positioning of the actor's hands. The music in this particular cabaret scene was titled "A Thousand Windows Smile at Me," and it was essential that I should prepare a pleasing, though not too flowery arrangement.

I spent the evening at home and on the task, and finally came up with not one but two contrasting arrangements. I felt it wise to hedge my bets! I arrived at Shepperton Studios the following morning at 10:00 a.m. in a state of considerable fear and trepidation. Perhaps at this point I should explain that ever since I had wrecked my neck playing the piano as a background for his silent films, Chaplin had to me seemed an almost godlike figure whose immense shadow on the silver screen was the only contact that ordinary mortals such as I could ever have hoped to have had with him. That I was now to actually meet him in the flesh and, what was more, that I might even be granted the incomparable honor of having the sound of my playing incorporated into one of his masterpieces, was a situation almost beyond comprehension. I began to wonder if the proper thing would be for me to pay him for the privilege!

Within minutes of reporting to "Reception" I was escorted to the studio where Mr. Chaplin, his wife, Oona, and Jerome Epstein, producer of *A King in New York*, were waiting to receive me. To my intense relief I observed that Chaplin was not twenty feet tall. Indeed he was quite a short man, probably no more than five-foot-six in height. I was also relieved by the cordiality of their reception and the fact that they were obviously trying to put me at ease. I think I must have been looking as nervous as I was feeling, and perhaps because of this he ordered an immediate showing on the screen of the appropriate clip. Directly after this was over he asked me to sit at the piano while the film was run through again so that I might rehearse one of my two transcriptions. After the sound of my playing had died away, Mr. Chaplin called out, "I'll buy that. That's exactly what I want." He followed it with some very nice compliments about my interpretation. I thanked him and said, "Well, when you are ready I'll do it again for real." I was astonished when they all laughed and explained that the microphones had been live and my playing was an actual "take." What an ego-trip that was—straight in the studio, no rehearsal, play the piece once and that was that. I could hardly believe it.

At this point the arranger of the film's music arrived and at Chaplin's request a part of the score was placed on the grand piano and I was asked to interpret it. Musicians will readily appreciate that in order to give a passable performance of an orchestral score on the piano it is necessary for one to be able to rapidly condense the vast number of separate staves into a basic melody and harmonic form that can be played with two hands. In the first instance, the melody has to be found and an immediate transposition made of some of the music written for the various orchestral instruments. Fortunately, being a quick reader and with considerable professional experience, I was able to make a passable interpretation within a few seconds.

When I had finished playing, Chaplin applauded and the word "formidable" issued from the lips of the French arranger, Boris Sarbek. I was very pleased, especially as I felt that I had in fact been undergoing a sort of audition. The time came to depart and Chaplin thanked and complimented me again. I felt that he really did appreciate my work, although in the back of my mind was the sneaking fear that it might be just "show biz sweet talk," agreeable to the ears but nothing more. Perhaps it was this that prompted me to say as we shook hands, "Mr. Chaplin, the nicest compliment that you can pay me is to ask me to work for you again." He smiled and said, "I will certainly do that," and as I turned and walked from the studio I felt that he really did mean it.

So my first meeting with Chaplin was over, and in the future I would be able to think of him, not as a large figure on a screen or indeed as a godlike figure, but rather as a smallish man of great presence. His snow-white hair capped a head that seemed disproportionately large for the relatively narrow shoulders that supported it. His hands were small and he used them most expressively. All in all he bore little resemblance to the comic figure that he portrayed so wonderfully on the screen.

As the months went by I began to feel more and more that the encounter with Chaplin would after all end up as a one-night stand and so I was quite bowled over when more than a year later I heard, on answering the phone, the voice of Jerome Epstein. He asked if I would be available to fly over to Switzerland in the next few days to work on some music with Chaplin in his home in Corsier, near Vevey. I need hardly say that I had no hesitation in accepting the assignment!

Air tickets and travel details were in my hands within twenty-four hours, and on a Sunday afternoon in October 1958 I boarded the plane at Heathrow and flew to Geneva, there to find a magnificent Continental Bentley, complete with a smart uniformed chauffeur, awaiting me. As the limousine conveyed me at high speed along the "autostrada" toward Vevey, I began to wonder if it was all just a dream and that I would shortly wake up in the office, having nodded off over the books! The distance to Vevey, which lies between Lausanne and Montreux, is about seventy kilometers; the road hugged the coastline of Lake Geneva and passed the hillside vineyards that overlook it. It was a beautiful journey and I was quite sorry when it ended at the further end of the town outside Hotel du Lac. In no time at all I was ensconced in a very large and comfortable bedroom with a private bathroom and a small balcony overlooking the lake.

I remember the time was exactly 4:00 p.m. and I was just about to unpack when the receptionist rang to say that Mr. and Mrs. Chaplin were awaiting me in the lounge. Feeling extremely flattered that the mountain had come to Mohammed, I sped off to join them. They greeted me most warmly, more like old friends than employers. This ability to treat people from all walks of life with the same respect and consideration was and still is a positive plus when I come to assessing the realities of the Chaplin legend. Never at any time did they talk down to me or make me feel second class. Our greetings over, they asked if I would like to have dinner with them that evening. It would have been a brave person who would have refused such an invitation. I was delighted and readily accepted. They smiled and expressed their pleasure and before leaving told me that the chauffeur would be at the hotel at 6:00 p.m. I was downstairs and waiting well before then, and promptly on the dot he arrived.

The journey on this occasion was about a mile to the little village of Corsier-sur-Vevey, a place full of character and charm and set on the hill overlooking the town of Vevey itself. Very soon the "Manoir de Ban," the Chaplins' home, came into view or just into view, because it was partly hidden by a number of large trees of many types. The road narrowed and shortly afterward we turned off onto a small parallel lane that took us to a wide gateway, through which we passed on to a large circular drive where a few seconds later we pulled up at the main entrance. The chauffeur opened the car door for me and as I walked toward the entrance the house door was opened by the butler, whose name I subsequently learned was Gino. He took my coat and then led me through a small hallway, which had three broad stairs leading to a pair of tall, glass-paneled doors. These in turn led into a very large hall where was situated a long refectory table on which stood several large models of nineteenth-century military figures.

From the hall a beautiful marble spiral staircase rose up toward the first floor. In the well of this staircase the wall was paneled to a height of about six feet with a curved mirror that effectively complemented the large display of flower arrangements. To the right of this was a spacious cloakroom, where the butler hung up my coat before taking me into the salon. Here I was greeted by the Chaplins as warmly as I had been at the hotel, and it was immediately suggested that Charlie take me on a tour of the house and estate. It was soon obvious that he enjoyed explaining the history of the Manoir and showing the considerable number of beautiful objects d'art that he had collected over the years. He also explained that apart from the fact that this tour might prove of interest to me, it was also essential that I should be completely orientated to what would be my working environment.

I was first taken through the large double doors at the end of the salon that led directly into the dining room, at the opposite end of which were similar doors that lead to Mr. Chaplin's study. This was oak-paneled with shelving on two sides, which contained masses of classic books on a great variety of subjects. Against one window was a desk that he had brought over from his Beverly Hills home. It was untidily covered with books and papers, as he spent a great deal of time sitting at it. I was quite surprised and delighted when he invited me to use this desk to work at whenever I wished. The study really was a delightful room, comfortable and warm and with a great deal of character.

The next stop was the room used exclusively by his secretary, Madame Eileen Burnier. Next to this was a chamber described as the garden room, which later became a second drawing room. Retracing our steps, we came to a place near the salon that appeared to be a large cupboard but when opened was shown to be a small lift for two persons. We went up in this to the first floor where he showed me his own private suite, which seemed almost spartan in its simplicity.

Further along the corridor we came to Mrs. Chaplin's private suite, the most fascinating aspect of which were two four-poster double beds. Immediately adjoining this room was a small and attractive boudoir off of which were a bathroom and a door leading to a paved sun patio. At the opposite end of the corridor was a large guest suite and on the opposite side were various other rooms.

Books were in evidence everywhere. It seemed as if every space that could take a shelf had been commandeered for this purpose. Mr. Chaplin explained that Oona was an avid reader and lover of good books.

The top or second floor consisted mainly of bedrooms for the children and their two nannies, plus several bathrooms and a linen room, the latter stacked from floor to ceiling with every kind of household linen.

On returning to the ground floor I was taken for a ten-minute walk through the gardens along the path, which wound its way among beautiful trees and shrubs. Mr. Chaplin told me that three circuits of this particular path measured exactly one mile and that he always endeavored to walk that distance at least once every day. At this point in his life he was still very active and usually played at least a couple of games of tennis before breakfast. He also made good use of the heated swimming pool and the fitness equipment attached to it.

Near the pool was a vegetable garden from which came all the vegetables used in the house throughout the year. I was also shown the large, thermostatically controlled greenhouse with shutters that opened and closed according to the prevailing temperature. From here came an unending supply of fruits and flowers in and out of season. The magnificent trees of every species were the outstanding features of the grounds and Mr. Chaplin explained that it was thanks to the former owner's obsession with the planting of rare specimens. Every year a delegation from the Horticultural and Botanical Society visited the Manoir to inspect the trees and shrubs to make certain that they were properly cared for and so preserved for posterity. He told me that in order to maintain the grounds in superb condition, he had to employ three full-time gardeners, headed by a conscientious gentleman named Walter.

We now returned to the salon, which was an extremely beautiful room, and a particularly well-heated one as it not only received the benefit of the central heating that was to be found throughout the house, but it had a log fire burning as well. Mr. Chaplin felt the cold very much and so a log fire was always lit in any room in which he proposed to spend some time.

There were far too many objects of interest and beauty around for me to describe now; however, I must mention the large crystal chandelier, the exquisite Adams mirror, and the beautiful marble chimneypiece. Also in the room were numerous framed pictures of family members and close family friends, and again lovely flower arrangements. For me, however, the most wonderful thing was the extremely beautiful Steinway grand piano in rosewood.

Mrs. Chaplin invited me to sit down, and I did so, carefully avoiding the two armchairs that I correctly judged to be no-go areas for anyone but the Chaplins. I sat on the settee, thankful not to have made a "faux pas" on my first visit. An aperitif was served and enjoyed and then dinner was announced.

I was placed to the left of Mrs. Chaplin and I thus faced Mr. Chaplin who straightaway expressed the hope that I liked chicken stew with small dumplings. I confessed that I had never sampled it and he retorted that it was too late for me to pull out now! In fact

I thoroughly enjoyed it and the fresh vegetables from the estate, the smoked ham and fresh sliced peaches, Swiss cheeses, fruits, and good local wine.

We returned to the salon for coffee and my confidence grew that working for Chaplin couldn't be at all bad if that was an example of the meals I could expect. Needless to say the immediate topic of conversation was music, and he put on a recording of Pablo Casals rehearsing the Brandenburg Concerto. Apparently Casals was unaware that the recording was being made and so one heard his uninhibited shouting and singing of various passages as he struggled to get what he wanted from the orchestra. It was quite hilarious. Chaplin's stereo equipment was truly of the best, with the loud speakers cunningly installed and completely hidden from view. They gave wonderful, almost three-dimensional effects. At 9:00 p.m. I suggested that it might be a wise thing if I returned to the hotel for a good night's sleep so that I would be ready to give of my best the following morning. Mr. Chaplin expressed his delight that I should put work before pleasure and said that if that were my attitude he was sure we would get along fine together! The chauffeur whisked me back to the hotel and I was soon in bed and asleep after what had been a long and most exciting day.

CHAPTER 2

$\mathcal{T}$he next morning the Bentley collected me at 9:45 a.m. I arrived at the Manoir at about 10:00 a.m. and was greeted by Mr. Chaplin with, "Good morning young man." Being forty-four years old at the time I felt that if all else had failed he would have done well in the diplomatic service! Incidentally he later asked me how old I thought he was. I, of course, already knew, so in reply I said that I felt it unwise for anyone in their mature years to ask that question as it might be taken to imply that they were merely seeking reassurance by being told they looked younger than they really were. He look a bit irritated at first, then smiled and said, "Of course you're right, Eric." I am quite sure that he never asked that question of anyone again.

Now, for the first time, Mr. Chaplin explained to me the nature of the work. It was simply that he was fed up with the "Mickey Mouse" type of accompaniment that was played so frequently to his silent films and that, with my help, he intended to compose suitable music to be recorded by a fifty- to sixty-piece orchestra. The first three films on which he wished to work were *A Dog's Life, Shoulder Arms*, and *The Pilgrim,* which were to be rereleased with an orchestral music track, under the composite title *The Chaplin Revue.* He went on to explain that 16mm copies of the films were being printed from the 35mm originals held in Denham Studios.

Unfortunately, these working prints had not yet arrived, so I suggested that it would be helpful if he would explain a little more about the films. What followed was one of the most memorable half hours that I have ever spent with him. He explained that we were to work on *Shoulder Arms* first and he promptly began to tell the story and illustrate it right there in the salon with the furniture as props. Most of the picture took place in the trenches during the First World War and he used the settee as a dug out and a walking stick as a rifle. From thence on he dodged imaginary shells, stumbled and crawled about the floor on his stomach and virtually reenacted the entire film. It was unforgettable and I was completely exhausted with laughing.

At the end of this crazy session he threw himself onto the piano stool, hit a sequence of notes and said, "That's the sort of melody with which I want to open this film." At this point I must mention something that may surprise a lot of people, namely that Charlie Chaplin could not play the piano well or read or write music, and knew very little about the theory and technicalities of music. Indeed, this was why he needed a music associate or amanuensis. He was able to use the first three fingers of the right hand to play sufficient notes to indicate the type of tune that was in his mind and that was usually enough for me to understand, providing he didn't try to bring in his left hand, when the resultant discords made it necessary for me to ask him to repeat the exercise one handed.

My job, after listening to the notes he had played on the piano as a basic melody line, was to formulate them into an acceptable musical composition, which I would then play back to him complete with chords and harmony. Hopefully, he would accept it. If not, he would ask me to try again or to emphasize this or that aspect of the melody and harmony or to change the mood and so on.

This was a tremendous challenge because his first thoughts were virtually random jottings of his melodic ideas, and bore little or no resemblance to the finished product. An hour or more would frequently be spent on perhaps one or two bars of the music until eventually his face would light up with a smile and he would say, "I'll buy that" (the only "Americanism" I ever heard him use during my long association with him).

I always kept about a dozen soft lead pencils lined up beside an enormous pile of manuscript paper plus a large eraser, which was in constant use! Melodic ideas were written down time and time again. This was owing to the fact that his dexterity with his three fingers on the keyboard of the piano did not match that of the creative side of his brain. Wrong notes would resound unceasingly when he played. Nevertheless, I always endeavored to write everything down since he would rarely follow a melodic thought through to its logical conclusion. It was extremely difficult to transcribe his compositions onto paper, particularly in the early stages of our association, before I appreciated the full importance of the part I needed to play in order that his ideas might be interpreted and made into an acceptable music score.

Fortunately, I have a quick ear and that did help in getting a basic melody onto paper. I remember when we were doing a piece of music called "Flat Feet" and working "blind" because the copy of *Shoulder Arms* had still not arrived, I wondered what a mess it would be when it came to fitting it to the particular "trench" sequence. However, when the copy did turn up and it was projected on to the screen, the music fitted the mood and movement of Chaplin to perfection. Needless to say we were both very pleased.

We must have presented a comic sight while at work because we would constantly be changing places at the piano. He would try to indicate with his limited playing ability what he was after and I would immediately change places and try to create the melody line that I felt he was searching for. It was like a game of musical chairs!

Another method he used to convey his musical thoughts to me was to sing. Unfortunately his singing was usually as out of tune as his playing and I used to dread this form of composition. He also was inclined to sing his melodies far more quickly than it was possible for me to transcribe them on paper. Patience was not one of Chaplin's virtue and he would frequently shout, "Haven't you got it down yet?" My reply was always the same: "I am a musician not a magician. I can only write music at a speed which is anatomically possible." I usually then added, "If you will sing a little slower I'll be able to keep up with you." He would then apologize and we would continue on and make good progress for a while at least.

He considered himself a perfectionist in everything and not the least where music was concerned. Frequently, days of concentrated work produced only two or three minutes of original composition a day. The music would be rewritten over and over again until finally we had reached a point when the entire composition was finished. When I played it back to him ostensibly for the last time, he would yet again start to make alterations. He would alter a couple of bars from one stave, then perhaps three from the stave below and one from the stave above and so on. Quite often I would cry "Stop" just in order to rest my mind for a few minutes and to give me the opportunity to rewrite the music yet again!

I think it was this aspect of working with Chaplin that caused many of my predecessors to walk out of the salon. When he told me of these occasions he added (perhaps as a warning) that as they made to leave he told them, "When you leave this room you will never, and I mean never, set foot in it again!" It was the memory of this that made me grit my teeth on many occasions and suffer the arguments and bullying that happened so frequently.

Each day followed the same regular pattern. We would commence at 10:00 a.m. and continue until lunchtime at 12:30 p.m. Then Mrs. Chaplin would enter the salon and almost invariably Mr. Chaplin would say, "Mummy, listen to the music that Eric and I have done this morning." The inclusion of my name in the composition made me smile inwardly but I would at once sit down and play the piece through.

In case the reader may gain the impression that it was I and not Mr. Chaplin that composed all the music, I should point out that the moment I was found acceptable for the job I was obliged to sign a legal document in which I was bound never to claim authorship of any music whatsoever that was created while working with Mr. Chaplin. In view of this I am of course prevented from suggesting otherwise and I most certainly would not wish to fall short of the law by so suggesting now. On every occasion, until he became too ill to cope with it, he would sing or try to show me "one fingerwise" at the piano in which direction his thinking lay and I merely used my musical talents to interpret this and produce from it a melody that was acceptable to him. As he remarked when he told me that I had to sign this declaration, "Where there's a hit, there's a writ, so it is best to confirm once and for all in writing to whom all compositions *must* be attributed!"

Lunch was always a simple meal, although wine was served. I always took beer so that I might keep a clear head for the afternoon sessions. We took coffee in the salon and while relaxing over it we chatted about current events and so forth but never about music. Promptly at 2:00 p.m. Mr. Chaplin would stand up and by so doing indicate that we should get on with the long stretch of four hours that lay ahead without a break until 6:00 p.m. I must say that I found this part of the day very tiring and after I had been working at the Manoir for a few days I ventured to ask if he ever stopped work for a cup of tea during the afternoon. He snapped back, "I'm sorry, but I don't like tea." Feeling this to be a bit lacking in consideration, I retorted equally, "Well, I do." To my surprise instead of a lordly rebuke he said quite gently, "How thoughtless, you must forgive me, Eric." He at once rang for Gino and from that day and every day thereafter a gentle tap would be heard on the door at precisely 4:00 p.m. and Gino would appear with a silver tray containing a pot of tea, a wedge of chocolate cake, and an assortment of sweet biscuits. At this point Mr. Chaplin would always insist that I should enjoy it while it was fresh and would then absent himself from the room for five minutes. Occasionally he would remain, sitting in the armchair facing me and I would feel waves of suppressed irritation wafting over as he tapped his fingers on the arm of his chair and dared me with his eyes to linger a moment longer than he considered necessary.

I discovered very early in my association with him that he was a glutton for work. Apart from lunch and the very brief tea break, we worked continuously from the moment I arrived at the Manoir until at least 5:30 p.m. I found it most exhausting trying to maintain the high degree of concentration and general efficiency that was expected of me. It was with tremendous sense of relief that I would hear him say, "Eric, I think we have done enough for today." There were occasions when he would add, "You have cheek, I think, keeping me at it the whole day," and he would end up by giving the impression that it was I who was slave driving and not him. He never seemed to understand that although younger, I, too, was utterly exhausted not the least by the frequent illustrations of his fiery temperament. When we did reach this moment he would go upstairs to his suite to rest and change for dinner while I continued the enormous amount of revision and rewriting.

During the day he would switch from one composition to another, making endless alterations and amendments and all this had to be attended to before my day was finished because he would expect a concert performance to which he would listen critically. Woe betide me if there was the slightest deviation from the melodic or harmonic pattern that he claimed had been agreed upon.

As it began to dawn on me what a very hard and demanding task master he was, I realized that my ability as a musician had to be balanced by my ability to suffer all silently, to maintain the patience of Job, and to be a super diplomat. He resented having to accept my advice at any time and when at the beginning I simply told him what was right he would shout, "Don't tell me what to do!" and I would have to wait until he reproduced my suggestions later and we could then get on.

I ultimately decided to simply play the correct thing and say, "How clever of you to think of that." It saved time and face! At times he could be quite difficult and I began to wonder if I were equal to the task. Certainly I now really understood why other musicians had left the salon forever, after only a few days.

Likewise my adoring attitude to the great Charlie Chaplin, which had remained with me from my boyhood days, disappeared rather rapidly and although I continued to admire him for his work, I realized that in other directions he was no better than any other man and probably a good deal worse than some.

His one redeeming feature was his ability to acknowledge his shortcomings. After I had been there about a week he turned to me after we had finished work one evening and said, "Eric, you must try not to be too upset by the things I say to you whilst we are working. I find that whenever I am doing creative work I am drawing on my nervous energy and seem unable to prevent myself from making these emotional outbursts." It was this self-effacing statement plus many other apologies thereafter that gave me the strength to endure the daily sessions, and it indeed gave me a deeper understanding of my employer and preserved my otherwise wilting respect for him. Perhaps it was this extra something within me that I was able to draw upon, that enabled me first to stay when others had left and then to go on for twenty years, during which time a genuine friendship existed between us.

An illustration of Mr. Chaplin's inability to retain a musical associate came when the receptionist at the Hotel du Lac inquired of me after only three days how long I would be staying. I was completely taken by surprise and the following morning got in contact with Madame Burnier, Chaplin's secretary, and asked her if she could explain. She laughed and said that there had been a great deal of embarrassment and expensive cancellation fees at the hotel when rooms had been reserved for a month for musicians who had left after only two or three days. As a precaution against an expensive repetition of these incidents, my employer had instructed that the hotel booking should be made for three days only. Madame Burnier assured me that Mr. Chaplin was more than satisfied in my case and had said that my room was to be reserved for a month. In point of fact I remained for six and a half weeks and I felt very flattered.

Sometimes after lunch we would take coffee on the long paved patio that overlooked the sloping lawns and the Dent du Midi. It was an exquisite location and the Chaplins had chosen it because of its peace and serenity, which was so essential for creative work. However, nothing is perfect and there were occasions when the peace of the Manoir would be shattered by enormous explosions and small arms fire, because detachments of the Swiss Army carried out military exercises in an area quite close to the estate's boundaries. This was usually on Tuesday afternoons and when it happened I was led to the conclusion that whatever day the estate agent originally showed the Chaplins the house it was definitely not a Tuesday. As the room shook with the vibrations of the explosions, Mr. Chaplin would stand at the window loudly cursing them and becoming so bad tempered that I was always glad when the day was over.

Never a day went by without arguments or disagreements over this or that passage of music. I soon found that it was virtually impossible for me ever to win, even when I could show the truth by demonstrating the musical correctness on the piano. I would get so frustrated that when Mrs. Chaplin saw me in this state she would encourage me to stand up to her husband and not to keep giving way. However, experience soon taught me the utter futility of trying to struggle through the verbal torrent of uninformed opinion, in order that I might persuade him to recognize the infallibility of musical law. I found it far easier to simply comment, "If I were you, no doubt I would say the same." This slightly impertinent comment would usually bring the incident to an abrupt end with more apologies at the end of the day.

There were several signs that gave warning of a rough session ahead. One of these was a pair of white cotton gloves. Every so often he suffered a mild form of eczema and when this occurred he wore these gloves as a form of protection. Alas, the sight of him wearing them inevitably indicated that he would be bad tempered and difficult to work with. It was on just such an occasion that he greeted me affably enough but suggested quite sharply that we should get right on with the work, indicating, or so it seemed to me, that I needed pushing.

In view of the fact that I devoted every waking moment to the job both in his presence and out of it, I seethed inwardly but bit my tongue. We progressed tortuously through the morning, during which nothing I did or suggested seemed right and every bar had to be analyzed and criticized. It was with heartfelt relief that I heard Gino announcing that lunch was ready and I hoped that after a good meal he might be in a better frame of mind. My hopes were dashed when on resuming work he at once began to again criticize everything I had done. At last, feeling my temper getting the better of me, I got up from the piano, walked across the room, and stood by the window clasping my hands to my head and slowly and deliberately counted to myself in an effort not to say something out loud for which I'd be sorry. Mr. Chaplin reacted immediately and walked to the piano, closed the lid on the keys, and said, "I think we'll stop work for today. We are just not on the same wavelength."

He walked rapidly to the door where he paused and turned. I thought, "He is now going to tell me the time of the next flight back to England." He didn't speak, however, but just glared, turned again, and passed through the door, which he closed with unnecessary force.

I felt deeply humiliated and almost running back to the piano I began to play loudly anything that came into my head. After a minute or two of this I felt decidedly better and began more calmly to run through the morning's work. About ten minutes had gone by when the door was suddenly opened again and the head and shoulders of my employer appeared. He gazed at me for a few seconds and then with the wistful smile of the "little fellow" on his face, he said, "Have you ever eaten a barbecue steak?" Thoroughly taken aback I managed a hesitant, "No, never." He gave a typical Chaplin sniff and said, "Well, you are going to tonight," and he was gone, the door closing more reasonably this time. He left me subdued but strangely happy and I set to work on the checking with renewed vigor.

At 6:00 p.m. the butler entered the salon to ask what I would like to drink and I was shortly afterward joined by Mrs. Chaplin. We both sat by the roaring log fire enjoying our aperitifs when it occurred to me that Mr. Chaplin was late in joining us for his predinner gin and tonic. I asked Oona if she knew what had happened to delay him. She grinned and said, "Take a look out of the window." I got up and was quite unprepared for the sight that met my eyes. There, on a spot close to the staff quarters, stood a large portable barbecue they had brought from their home in California. Mr. Chaplin was garbed in a very heavy Crombie overcoat with its collar turned up to meet the rim of the black Homburg that had been pulled down well over his ears. He was gently turning the steaks and large jacket potatoes in between bouts of foot stamping and hand slapping, which, because of the extreme cold of this November evening, was so necessary in spite of the heat from the barbecue fire.

I felt deeply concerned that he should be exposed to such conditions and asked Mrs. Chaplin if I could go and help him. Mrs. Chaplin immediately replied, "No, Eric, don't go outside. Just leave him alone. This is his way of saying he's sorry for being such a pig to you today." I was deeply touched and felt that however difficult or unreasonable he would undoubtedly be in the future, this indication of a real and sensitive human being lurking within would help me to weather the storms and accept that this was part of the job.

I might add that the meal was excellent. I have never had a better one and when at the end of it I was told that all the family would find it agreeable if from thence on I referred to them by their first names, I felt that I had really arrived. It had been a bittersweet day but it was the beginning of our long and mainly happy association.

As I have already mentioned, he would convey his wishes to me by singing, humming, or three-fingered playing on the piano. It was amazing how, from this, music would emerge that was both acceptable and correct, fitting to the mood of the pictures. He always wanted music that was tuneful even if a little old-fashioned. He once commented that if the public didn't like his picture they should be able to close their eyes and enjoy the music! He often carried about him a simple cassette recorder, which he would use whenever I was not with him.

His other method of committing to memory some melody that might suddenly come to him was extremely bizarre. He would jot down on paper the names of established pieces of music that contained the notes he required. For instance he might put down "first two notes of Grieg's 'Morning,'" "next four notes, those in the opening bars of Liszt's 'Liebestrmäume,'" another three bars from something else and so on and so on. Later he would give me the list and I would notate them on sheet music and begin to create the melody I felt he had in mind. It was the most arduous and difficult way I've ever heard of in music composition. I always felt quite amazed that Charlie, with all his talents, had never taken the trouble to acquire the elementary knowledge of music that would have saved the agony of the foregoing, and made life a good deal easier, and maybe done away with the need to employ a musician like me!

Charlie would always voice his opinion as to which instrument in the orchestra should be given the various passages of the music. "This phrase," he would say, "must be given to the violins, and we must have a cello obbligato with it," or, "Let us give this phrase to the woodwind and then throw it to the brass," and so on, until every phrase had been allocated.

Charlie was not a lover of the brass section but preferred the strings, and in particular the cellos. He would have used them in every conceivable passage of the music had I not taken a firm stand and pointed out that their repetitious use would destroy the validity of all that we had done.

I was also, from time to time, able to prevent him making an even graver error, that of unintentional plagiarism. Now and then he would greet me in the morning with a happy smile and, switching on his little tape recorder, eagerly study my face as he played over the outline of a melody. Often at the end he would glower and say, "I can see by your face that you don't think much of it." I would reply, "On the contrary Charlie, I think it's absolutely wonderful but what a pity that Tchaikovsky thought of it before you did."

His face would fall and he'd say, "I've been working on that melody for more than two hours and you've destroyed it in two seconds." I always replied the same: "Two seconds disappointment now is better than years of embarrassment later."

Once when I suggested to him that he should have taken time off to study harmony and counterpoint, he replied that he preferred to think freely, like a gypsy, and not be hemmed in by all the music rules and inhibitions by which most musicians are governed. As I swallowed hard and sought desperately for a reply, he added, quite apart from all else, "If I had been as knowledgeable as a musician, I would not have had the pleasure of working with

Eric James." There seemed no answer to that, so I left the subject! Perhaps if he had understood a bit more about the technicalities he would not have dictated countless ideas and melodies to me with the speed of a machine gun, which were almost impossible to cope with and resulted in considerable tidying-up work for me each day.

I must say my employment with Charlie was a labor of love, because the financial reward was out of all proportion to my value to him. In the first instance I had only myself to blame. I had been there about a week, when Charlie suddenly turned to me and said, "Perhaps you'll be good enough to ring my business manager, Miss Rachel Ford, in her Paris office and tell her what you require as remuneration for your services. I leave all money matters to her as I don't wish to have relationships hampered by time consuming mundane discussions about money." I was taken completely off my guard and being at that time still somewhat besotted with Charlie Chaplin, I foolishly adopted the attitude that working for and being with him was such an honor that it was a reward in itself. I thus asked and received a very nominal figure.

In view of the fact that the various films that I worked on with him have netted some millions, a more generous increase in my salary would hardly have put him on the road to bankruptcy. The legal document I had signed disclaimed any rights to the compositions. It also prohibited me from receiving any royalties from the music or any pecuniary advantage whatsoever over and above my salary. I would be less than honest if I did not say that I feel disappointed about this. Quite apart from the undoubted legality of my position, I think that I should have received some solid recognition as a purely voluntary gesture.

It may well be that Charlie never knew at any time what I was being paid, but over a period of twenty years that does seem unlikely. As a matter of interest, I started working for him for £60 ($120.00) a week, that being the sum I myself had asked. Thereafter my remuneration was raised from time to time by Rachel Ford without recourse to me until after twenty years of service I was receiving £200 ($400.00). It must also be remembered that I was not working with Charlie every week of the year but unlike many other persons on his payroll, I was never paid a retainer.

I can only conclude that business and friendship were two distinct things in Charlie's eyes. Many of the people who had met

Charlie have subsequently indicated they found him to be a less than generous individual, and indeed my own experience bears that out.

It has also been suggested that his meanness in later life stemmed from his early experiences when he lived in conditions of such poverty that it left him permanently scarred. He would often talk to me about his early life and would express a deep-felt fear that he might one day find himself back in a similar situation. Much as I wanted to, I could never quite accept this statement (in spite of his saying that he could not be bothered with mundane money matters), that he could not have failed to appreciate the fact that the amount of money he possessed and the constant income from royalties, etc., was such that he could not possibly—even in the longest lifetime imaginable—have returned to a state of poverty.

However, working with Charlie did have bonuses of another sort and one such occurred on a Friday afternoon when I was asked if I would like to join the family party after dinner the next evening, in order to attend a performance of the famous "Circus Knie." Apparently this circus came to Vevey once a year to give a special show, and it always occurred toward the end of their touring season. The big top was erected in the famous Market Square, the largest square on the continent and one on which Napoleon was said to be able to review his entire army.

The following evening, precisely at 7:45 p.m. three cars pulled away from the Manoir; they contained the complete party of ten: Oona, Charlie, Geraldine, Michael, Josephine, Victoria, Eugene, the two nannies, affectionately known as Kay Kay and Pinnie, and, of course, myself. Very shortly afterward we arrived at the entrance to the circus, where, resplendent in top hat and tails and bright red carnation, Mr. Knie himself stood waiting to greet us. The minute we stepped from the cars, my ears were filled with the sound of the circus orchestra and I was taken back in my mind to Eric the choir boy attending the annual church outing to Bertram Mills circus. That boy, in his wildest dreams, would never have imagined visiting a circus with Charlie Chaplin and his family.

The music created the same exciting anticipation and it was a happy party that was led to the edge of the ring. As we entered the big top all the main lights were dimmed and at the same moment a powerful spotlight in the upper rigging snapped into life and focused straight on Charlie, who stopped as if in surprise. The sound of the music changed to the opening bars of "Eternally" from the film *Limelight*. At this, the entire audience of over two thousand people rose to their feet clapping, stamping, and shouting "Charlot, Charlot." Charlie continuously lifted his hands in acknowledgment and turned several times to look at Oona.

From his face I could see that although this could not be a new experience for him, he was nevertheless deeply moved. Every light was blazing now, enabling me to see the sincerity on the faces of all these people, young and old, as they gave this spontaneous demonstration of their feelings. Nearly four minutes passed before we were able to take our places in the reserved enclosure, and I was thankful that we could do so as the whole episode was very emotional. The lights were lowered and there began a wonderful show in which some of the world's finest specialty acts performed. At the end of it Mr. Knie came forward and invited us to his caravan. We all walked outside and the two nannies departed for home with the three youngest children, leaving us to be escorted through to his travelling home.

Any thought that I shall now describe a little wooden structure on four wheels with shafts for a horse can be forgotten. What we were led to were three enormous ultra modern caravans linked together into a beautiful luxurious suite of rooms. Inside, food and drink had been laid out, and we were joined by all the artists that had taken part in the show. Luckily all of them understood English, to a greater or lesser degree, and so were able to listen with obvious pleasure as Charlie regaled them with amusing and entertaining reminiscences. There wasn't a dull moment. I can honestly say that I never saw him looking happier. He was no longer a world famous figure set apart, but a clown among clowns and an entertainer among entertainers. I was really sorry when after about two hours it was announced that our cars had arrived and this most memorable of evenings was over.

The days went by and gradually the music for the triple compilation film, *The Chaplin Revue*, began to take on a definite shape. The three films were all of varying length but together they totaled two hours and twenty five minutes. Incidentally, I should mention that in the film *The Pilgrim*, there was a special title song, "Bound for Texas" with lyrics by Charlie, and when this song was recorded it was sung by Matt Munro, who did a great job and was warmly congratulated by Charlie. As the music was to be continuous, it was an extremely formidable challenge and I often felt that I wouldn't be able to stay the course. To help me mentally and physically I kept up a daily routine. I would rise each morning at 7:30 a.m., take a shower and then enjoy a leisurely breakfast, after which I would have a brisk walk along the promenade of the lake, returning to the hotel by the main street of the little town. Thus by 9:30 I was fully awake and alert and ready to face the exhausting demands and mental acrobatics that Charlie would inevitably expect of me.

Charlie usually declared that he had done enough work for the day at about 5:30 and he would then take the lift upstairs, where he would have a bath or sauna and then reemerge at about 6:00 p.m. dressed in what he called his siren suit. As soon as he rejoined me, Gino would enter the salon to serve us drinks. Charlie always downed his gin and tonic at great speed and then was served a second, which he dealt with more slowly and usually made it last until dinner was served promptly at 6:45. Sometimes we would be joined by Josephine, aged nine, and always known as Josie, and Victoria, aged seven, and referred to as Vicky, though normally they took their evening meal with their nannies upstairs. Occasionally Eugene, aged five, known always as "Tadpole," would come into the room and that would indeed make a complete change from the day's musical activities.

Charlie and I would join in all the games and sometimes he would go down on all fours and pretend to be a growling bear. This resulted in screams of laughter and lots of running about. Although it has been suggested that the relationship in later years between the children and their father was not all that could have been wished, I can say from personal observation that Charlie gave them all the love and affection that any father could have shown.

Clad in a long cocktail dress or a glamorous housecoat and with not a hair out of place, Oona would usually arrive right in the midst of all the pandemonium. When dinner was announced we took our places at what was always a beautifully laid dining table. Oona usually prepared the week's menus for Mary, the cook, and she rarely included a dish that was unlikely to please her husband.

However, on the occasions when Charlie declined what was offered to him, Oona never attempt to persuade him or suggest an alternative dish. She accepted that when he said, "No, thank you," he meant it. She once indicated to me that a part of her diplomacy in maintaining their wonderfully happy life together was to accept that "no" meant "no" and not to irritate him by trying to make him change his mind.

It was at dinner, after six and a half exhausting weeks that had seen the completion of the pianoforte scores, that Charlie announced there would be a final run through of the music after the meal was over. Charlie settled himself in his favorite armchair and Oona carried out her usual task of being the projectionist, while I began to give a concert performance. I had to punctuate the music by loudly exclaiming the various orchestral annotations while at the same time watching the film very closely so that I might change the various pieces of music at the prearranged cues.

It gave me a tremendous sense of satisfaction to observe how perfectly the music fitted the various scenes in the films. As the last notes died away, Charlie, positively beaming with pleasure, got to his feet, put his hand on my shoulder and said, "Eric, you've done a good job. You may write your own screen credit." I hesitated and then cheekily suggested, "Music written and composed by Eric James in spite of Charlie Chaplin." Fortunately, he laughed heartily and I subsequently suggested, "Eric James—Music Associate." Charlie accepted this immediately and said, "It shall be a half plate credit and it shall follow my own full plate credit." The length and timing of the film footage for the credit were quite considerable, usually around 15 seconds, and they have remained unaltered for all the films on which I have worked with Charlie.

And so my first stint at Vevey was over and I returned home to England carrying with me a heavy load of music, a lot of happy memories, plus a large photograph of Charlie, which he presented to me and on which he had written, "To Eric with many thanks for your patience and understanding." I had certainly needed patience and understanding and I was glad that he acknowledged the fact.

CHAPTER 3

One immediate result of my work with Chaplin was that Michael Parkinson of the BBC gave me carte blanche to negotiate an interview with him. My request met with point blank refusal. He said that he wanted no further publicity except perhaps for a reasonable amount whenever he launched a new picture. No special interviews would ever be granted to BBC, newspapers, or magazines for he resented being asked "loaded" questions. As time went by I came to realize that he could not forget or forgive the treatment he had frequently received from much of the world's media.

The end of the work in Switzerland merely marked the beginning of the work in England. There was an enormous amount to be done and for this I had the cooperation of Eric Spear, a fine musician, and incidentally the composer of the theme music for the *Coronation Street* television series. We had to get all the piano scores orchestrated and copied, and Eric Spear was meticulous in noting all the various annotations and orchestral suggestions made on my pianoforte scores during the sessions in Vevey.

It was just as well to get things right, as Charlie constantly insisted that I write down his wishes and carry them out to the letter. He told me that he did not wish to waste valuable time in the recording studios correcting errors because I had failed to make proper notes. He would always end this dissertation with, "Studio time is expensive and so I warn you—be accurate." There was little doubt that it was just the expense that worried him.

As one who has never been very rich, it has always puzzled me why those who have no money worries whatsoever should count every penny, especially when, in this case, I was told by Charlie, when referring to my salary, that he did not bother himself with mundane money matters. In point of fact it was an extreme rarity indeed for any of my work to need rescoring in the studio. Many, many, hours were spent discussing with the other Eric the most effective way of orchestrating the enormous amount of music that I had brought back to England. We also had to decide what would be the ideal combination of instruments to bring out the vast musical sound, taking into account Charlie's marked preference for the strings. We finally came up with eight woodwind, eight brass, two percussion, harp and piano, and thirty-one strings—a total of fifty-one musicians with the option to augment in the case of special arrangements. Charlie approved this setup without hesitation and we were able to begin engaging the finest available players.

The studio at Denham was reserved for a minimum of ten three-hour sessions to follow many weeks of the preliminary work. As it turned out I had correctly estimated the time needed, and the two hours and twenty-five minutes of continuous music was duly completed in that time in spite of the multiple alterations that Charlie still insisted on making, even though this or that small adjustment kept the entire orchestra immobile for long periods.

It was quite an ordeal standing with Charlie in the control box at the moment when Eric Spear lifted his baton to conduct the first recording of music that hitherto had only been heard when I had played it on Charlie's piano. Happily for me he was delighted and demanded no further changes. Oona and Jerome Epstein were also in the box and both gave unstinted approval. One policy we adopted to cope with Charlie's inevitable interventions was to deliberately cue in the melody lines for alternative instruments when scoring; this was a tremendous saving of time when we were called upon to make last minute changes. This system of arranging the music in a more or less foolproof way, applied throughout my long association with Charlie, was adopted by every arranger I engaged to make the orchestral score. It was a joy working with Eric Spear and his death sometime later was quite a shock. I then invited Lambert "Bill" Williamson to work with me. He was most cooperative and efficient in his writing but was unfortunately ultimately obliged to retire owing to ill health, but not before he had done a great deal of work with me on the completion of the music for *A Countess from Hong Kong* in 1966 and *The Circus*, which was recorded in 1968.

It was at this point some ten years after first working for Charlie that yet another Eric, Eric Rogers, came to partner me in the work.

From the very outset it was a most agreeable association, both through his competence as a musician and his likeable personality. We continued working together most successfully until Charlie died in 1977. During this period we had cooperated on six films: *The Kid*, *The Idle Class*, *A Day's Pleasure*, *Pay Day*, *Sunnyside*, and *A Woman of Paris*. I can honestly say that *The Kid* was my favorite of all the Chaplin's films on which we worked. The music was quite operatic in parts and complemented the contrasting scenes perfectly. There was a truly delightful theme, which was effectively scored mainly featuring the string section of the orchestra and a lyric was subsequently written and become known as "I Walk the Streets." Then followed *The Idle Class*, which from then on was always paired with the screening of *The Kid*. In 1973 we recorded the music for *Pay Day* and later in the same year we did *A Day's Pleasure*. In 1974 I worked with Charlie on *Sunnyside* and it was obvious that he was beginning to run out of original ideas for the music. As a result it was decided that for the final sequence of the film we would use a melody from Balfe's operetta *The Bohemian Girl,* and a credit to this effect was duly included in the opening captions. The final film I worked on with Charlie was *A Woman of Paris*, which was recorded in 1976.

I have tried to describe something of my feelings engendered by my first visit to Vevey in 1958. It was a great experience and when it was ended I had no guarantee that it would all be repeated. It is true that we got on well and he liked me, but my greatest hopes were for, perhaps, a spasmodic engagement. I certainly never for one moment imagined that our association was to last twenty years, and that I should make the journey to Vevey some forty times. The six and a half weeks we had spent together, locked in musical battle, had been enough for both of us to learn a great deal about the other. Working with him was something like walking on a tightrope that was constantly being shaken and made me all the more determined not to fall off. Charlie, oddly enough, seemed to respect me because of this.

The fact that I had also reached a point where I refused to be kicked around and did not hesitate to criticize or answer him back also seemed to earn me a grudging admiration, in spite of the fact that it was doubtless a new experience for him. All this, plus the knowledge that I now understood the true dimensions of the work I had to do, made the next visit and all those thereafter so much easier in every way. As time went by I really did feel like one of the family and was treated by all as such.

Whenever I returned to the Manoir I was always greeted in a way that bore no relationship to that of employee and employer. Their greetings were warm and sincere, and I would hardly have sat down before refreshments were served. I remember one occasion when circumstances made it impossible for me to reach the Manoir in time for lunch. I arrived long after the Chaplins had finished theirs, and I was sitting alone in the dining room waiting for Gino to serve me when I became aware of a slight sound in the adjacent salon. I turned and saw Chaplin with an old hat and scarf on, shoulders narrowed, back arched, head and hands shaking, staggering through the door with the aid of a stick as if he were an extremely old man. With an appropriate croaking ancient voice he asked, "Had a good flight my boy? Shall we do a bit of work after lunch, eh?" He then straightened up, discarded his hat, scarf, and stick, slapped me on the shoulder and said, "Glad to see you back, Eric." It was such a natural uninhibited action that I felt at home immediately, and not the least it indicated—correctly as it turned out—that he would be in a good mood for the rest of the day.

The children, who always referred to me as Uncle Eric, were all bilingual and frequently, when two or more met together, would lapse into French. If Oona were present they would be told immediately to revert to English. It was a rare occurrence for all five children to be present at any mealtime. When I inquired the reason, Charlie said that Oona and he had found that when all the children were together, it was bedlam, and no single child could be heard properly. They had decided, therefore, to put into operation a rota system so that each child in turn would be alone at the table and thus able to receive a proper hearing and undivided attention. The system worked extremely well.

The feeling of being part of the family was greatly enhanced by the freedom I had been given to treat the house as if it were my own, and to wander where I wished as any other member of the family would. It gave me a great sense of belonging and enabled me to work free from any actual or mental restriction. I loved using the desk in Charlie's personal study and would always go there to do my work unless Charlie was using it to write his autobiography, which he did from time to time over a period of seven years. On these occasions I would instead sit at the enormous desk that he had brought with him from his home in Beverly Hills and that was situated in the second drawing room. This room too, had large windows that gave plenty of light and at this period of my life I desperately needed all the light I could get, as I was having a great deal of trouble with my eyesight, sufficiently so that I got quite depressed and had great fears for my vision in the future— luckily as it turned out unfounded.

As time went by Charlie would also worry over health considerations, especially when they were of a "tempus fugit" nature. All his life he had expressed disdain for people who took a nap after lunch but finally he began to do so himself. The need for him to have this period of relaxation during the day was something beyond his own control but he felt desperately unhappy about it and frequently expressed to me how embarrassed he felt. I tried to console him with the fact that Winston Churchill, even during the war's most critical periods, not only went to bed after lunch but actually completely undressed to do so, which was more than Charlie ever did.

He was quite pleased to learn this, but never really accepted that he had reached this stage of life. However, every cloud has a silver lining and thanks to Charlie's afternoon siestas I was able to make good use of the well-heated outdoor swimming pool. Sometimes I would take manuscript paper and pencil in order to sort out knotty musical problems between dips. Invariably at about 3:00 p.m. I would hear in the distance the voice of Charlie calling, "Eric, Eric," and I would immediately dress and return to the salon, and work would begin again. These were much happier days and the rapport between us grew stronger all the time. We understood each other now and I was able to correctly sense and anticipate what Charlie was seeking musically.

The passing of time had also manifested itself on Charlie in another and perhaps more delicate way and it does enable me to relate a comic, if down to earth, aspect of his personality. It was quite a usual thing for us to take a walk through the gardens between sessions or in the evenings, and it was during one of these strolls early on in our acquaintance that Charlie suddenly said, "You know, Eric, another penalty of growing old is that I'm having trouble with my pisser. When I've got to go, I've got to go and I want to go right now. Is there anyone about?" Before I could answer him that all was clear he had rushed into the bushes and positioned himself by a large tree. The crude, though accurate, description of his difficulty quite startled me and when Charlie re-emerged, adjusting his clothing, he must have sensed my feelings because he said, "Trouble with me, Eric, is that although I've come a long way since my orphanage days some traces of that life have obviously remained."

The same sort of incident happened many times thereafter but never with any further comment. We would be walking along, perhaps discussing some musical matter when, perhaps in the middle of a sentence, he would be gone, quite often near the same tree. After a few seconds he would reappear and continue talking at exactly the same point just as if nothing had happened. I've often wondered if this recurrent activity had any adverse effect on the trees and amusing to consider what malady would have been ascribed by the members of the Horticultural and Botanical Society when they made their annual inspection. No doubt many an innocent termite or faultless fungi took the rap for Charlie's dispensations!

Tuesday at the manor was always known as "Congé," which meant that it was a day off for all the staff both inside and out, except for the butler who had his free day later in the week. This meant lunch elsewhere for me and I would duly be whipped off by taxi back to my hotel or a restaurant of my choice, and then be returned for the afternoon's work. When evening came, more often than not, Oona, Charlie, and myself would go out to dine at one of the many first-class restaurants in the vicinity. Quite often they would choose the small but delightful restaurant at St. Saphorin known as "Auberge de Londres," where one of the specialties of "la maison" was frogs' legs. The table would be reserved in advance and we were always attended by the proprietor, who was also the chef. Another popular venue was the famous "La Grappe d'or" in Lausanne, where the greatest task was to make a choice, as the menu was so vast. One of the specialties was fish; a large illuminated glass tank stood just inside the entrance. From it one could choose a fish that would then be cooked and served. Alas, in my book it is one thing to eat fish that has arrived from the fishmongers, already dead, and quite another to condemn to death a fish that is alive, well, and looking beautiful right there in front of one's eyes. My conscience never wavered and not one single fish ever received the thumbs down sign through me.

Although Charlie's gastronomical preferences at home were for rather simple dishes, he always, when dining out, chose more exotic things such as roast partridge or pheasant. He also liked good wine and this restaurant served only the best. On top of this, he usually plumped for caviar for starters. I used to get goose pimples thinking what these meals must have cost and shuddered at the thought of what would have happened if ever they left hurriedly, leaving me to pay the bill. I guess I would still have been there to this day, washing dishes! Oona always paid because Charlie never carried money.

On the rare occasions when for some reason or other it was decided that we should have dinner at home on a Tuesday, the butler's wife would always prepare an excellent meal.

Occasionally Charlie would lapse into a reminiscent reverie and I treasure the memory of those happy occasions. For one thing, it meant that he was in a good mood, but it also meant that he would become an ordinary person, completely uninhibited and divested of any lingering traces of "force de grandeur." Sometimes, when he was in this mood he would take from the drawer of the display cabinet a pile of his father's song copies, published by Francis, Day & Hunter Co. They included "Eh! Boys?" and "Oui! Tray Bong," typical songs of a Lion Comique of the British Music Hall. He always kept them there and I felt there was something symbolic about the choice of this location because above them, in the cabinet itself, was a collection of porcelain and objets d'art that were probably worth more than his father had earned in his whole lifetime by singing the very words and music printed on those old and tattered pieces of paper.

The sheets were in fact beautifully produced and to this day some people collect them. Highly colored and in caricature vein they usually displayed a likeness of an artist of the day, and many of them in fact depicted Charles Chaplin Sr. Charlie would always choose some, hand them over to me, and I would play and sing them, while he sat with eyes closed, quite happy but always with a hint of sadness on his face. He often complimented me on what he considered an amazing accomplishment, namely that I could coordinate the playing and yet read and sing the lyrics at the same time. I must say that this seemed a very elementary thing for any pianist to do, especially one like myself who had been a song plugger. I guess this illustrates yet again how little Charlie knew about the technicalities of music making.

There were other times when his reminiscing moods would take him to the realms of the old music halls and the great stars they produced: Vesta Tilley, "Little Tich," Marie Lloyd, Harry Champion, and many, many others. On these occasions he would invariably take up a position with his back to the chimneypiece while I sat at the piano. He would then turn, give a little bow in my direction, and say in a voice with cockney overtones, "Music, maestro, if you please." I would commence and he would begin to sing in the flamboyant style of the turn-of-the-century music hall of yesteryear and always be word perfect. He would then wave his hand to me to join in and the two of us would indulge in a good old-fashioned "sing-song," enjoying every minute of it, as did Oona or anyone else who happened to be within earshot.

While recalling Charlie's gift for "hamming up," in true music hall fashion, the songs of yesteryear, I must relate an incident that occurred during the time that we worked on the music for *The Circus,* which was to be conducted by Lambert "Bill" Williamson. Charlie asked me to arrange for someone who specialized in singing the current pop songs of the day. I contacted John McCarthy, who at that time was the conductor and arranger for the famous McCarthy singers, and he readily agreed to send three male vocalists to make a demo-record of the song at the Star Sound Studios in London. Charlie heard them and chose a singer whose name was Ken Barrie.

The song that was to be recorded was called "Swing High Little Girl," with lyrics by Charlie Chaplin, and this was to be sung while the opening credits were being projected. It proved to be extremely popular with Oona and the family, and Charlie would invariably burst into song whenever I played the introduction to it. His voice, as I have already revealed, was anything but good, and yet it sounded quite effective when he sang this particular song. Maybe it was because he gave a performance that resembled the way a music hall or vaudeville artist would sing it, so I decided that it might be a good idea to have a set of music parts written in his key just in case the contract vocalist didn't give the kind of treatment that was required for this number.

On the day that we subsequently had set aside for the recording session at the Anvil Studios, Denham in Buckinghamshire, I did not feel that the interpretation of "Swing High Little Girl" was the one that we were seeking and said to Charlie, "Wouldn't it be a nice idea if you were to make a recording so that Oona and all the family could enjoy hearing you sing 'Swing High Little Girl' with the backing of this lovely orchestra?" I went on to say, "I am sure they would appreciate your doing this for them." Needless to say he agreed that it would be an ideal opportunity to do so and thus it was that we immediately made the recording, with Charlie giving the song the same treatment that he had given so many times in his home in Vevey.

After hearing the playback, it was obvious that his rendition would be so much better suited to the film than the one that had been recorded earlier that morning by the contract singer, excellent as it was. I will always remember Charlie's words to me after all present agreed that it would be far better to use his recording for the opening of the film. He said, "Eric, you 'conned' me into doing that, didn't you?" I remember my reply, which was to the effect that had I suggested it in Vevey, he would have immediately refused on principle to make a recording and so in order to get my way I had to resort to a little subterfuge—which fortunately came off!

The first time I saw copies of the song "Eternally" from the film *Limelight*, I was amazed to see so many of them. Closer examination revealed them all to be different. They were in fact copies sent to him by the music publishers of the many countries that had published this hit song. I played them all at one time or another and it was quite amusing to find how different were the values of the note and the various arrangements of the accompaniment, although the melody line remained more or less the same. The difference between, say, the South American, Italian, Japanese, and English versions was quite astonishing.

During my first assignment with Charlie, I had the pleasure of meeting his famous half brother Sydney on a number of occasions. Together, as children, they had experienced the same soul-destroying poverty, the unhappiness of the family misfortunes, and the joyless interior of the orphanage—now, for him, as with Charlie, the pendulum had swung its full distance and he lived with his charming wife, Gypsy, in a lovely home in the south of France, lacking for nothing and far from the life and environment of the seedy neighborhood of childhood days.

At certain times every year, Sydney and Gypsy would live at the Hotel Beau Rivage in Lausanne. From there they would come to dinner at the Manoir once every fortnight, and on alternate Tuesdays, the Chaplin family, including myself, would dine with them at the Beau Rivage. The children really loved Uncle Sydney, for he was always very amusing and loved to play with them. Quite apart from anything else, Sydney was a good businessman and in his early days in Hollywood, Charlie relied on him absolutely when investing his money. Indeed, I was quite surprised when he told me that his income was almost entirely derived, not from royalties, sale of music and so on, but from the wise investments in gilt-edged securities and blue chips suggested by Sydney.

Unfortunately, by the time of my second assignment at Vevey, *A Countess from Hong Kong*, Sydney had died and so it was only unhappy Gypsy who continued the tradition of exchanging dinner parties. I remember her both for what she was, a very sweet person, and for her amusing habit of keeping her reading glasses on the top of her head, no matter what she was wearing and where she was. It was a bit odd but at least she always knew where they were!

One of my favorite film star pin-ups was Benita Hume, and I had the pleasure of meeting her at the Manoir. In my eyes she was still as radiant and lovely as ever and it was sad to think of the suffering she must have gone through when her husband, George Sanders, took his own life. Another tragic figure came to dinner one evening and it was a very sad occasion. I refer to Mrs. Tyrone Power, who had lost her husband only a few weeks previously when he had collapsed and died while working on a film in Spain.

In point of fact, hundreds of interesting people came to see Charlie during those twenty years that I worked with him, and if I started listing them now, this book would simply become a "Who's Who," which in my view is a boring aspect of many auto-biographies. However, I simply must mention one visitor. We were sitting together in the salon when Oona brought in a telegram. Charlie read it and passed it over to me without saying a word. It said, "Edwina and I will be passing through Switzerland on Friday this week. Will it be convenient for us to call?—Signed Mountbatten." Charlie was elated and flattered, not only because of the stature of both Mountbatten and his wife, but because they had actually asked if they could come and had not taken it for granted. To me it seemed just basic etiquette that they should have contacted him but not to Charlie, who floated on cloud nine.

Immediate confirmation followed of course, and preparations were made for the great day. When the event was over, Charlie would often refer to it and he regarded the visit as a very great honor, not only because Mountbatten was a member of the royal family but also because he was undoubtedly one of the truly great men of our times.

Thanks to Oona, who refused to let her husband and me work a seven-day week and who said that, quite apart from anything else, we needed to have at least one day away from each other, I was always free on Sundays when there was usually a large family gathering. If the weather was good, one could be sure of a barbecue on the grounds. Unfortunately I usually found that I had to spend a part of the day doing revision and writing the music composed during the previous week. Nevertheless, I made it a rule to always salvage a few hours during the day to go sightseeing. In this I was helped by Eileen Burnier and her husband, who on a number of occasions took me to see some of the most outstanding scenic areas of Switzerland.

With the passing of time and the strengthening of our friendship, I reached a point where I felt able to mention a subject, that, because of its implications, was a very touchy one indeed. I refer to the charge made against Chaplin by Senator Joseph McCarthy, that Charlie was a communist. This slur caused him a very great amount of real suffering, which was to leave its mark and ultimately to alter his whole way of life. Indeed he would have never come to Vevey, and for that matter I would not have become his music associate, had not Charlie been subjected to this abuse both from McCarthy and most of the media.

The McCarthy "witch hunt" seemed to be hell bent, without any real justification, to destroy him and indeed many other public figures, either on charges of communist sympathies or other anti-American behavior. I brought the matter up one evening while we were sitting on a bench in the garden. I turned to him and bluntly asked, "Tell me, Charlie, were you a communist?" He looked at me and for a moment made no answer. When he did, it was in a most reproachful manner. "Even you would wish to ask me that, Eric." I felt that perhaps I had gone too far and I expressed my regrets for having brought the subject up. He at once assured me that the matter was in no way banned, but he had had communism up to his neck and if I had suffered as much as he had done because of its unwarranted attachment to his name, I would doubtless feel just as frustrated as he did at never being able to shake himself free of it.

He looked at me almost desperately, "I can truly swear, Eric, that at no time have I been guilty of any charges relating to un-American activities, and that includes communism. If it had been otherwise I would tell you now and trust that our friendship would temper your reaction.

"I am in my own home and I don't have to defend myself to anybody and certainly not lie in order to do so. If you ask me have I any communist friends, then maybe I have, maybe you are one—how do I know? Your political views were never called into question when you were engaged to come and work with me. I accept people for far more important qualities than their religious and political beliefs and indeed, when I sum up a friend, integrity and sincerity come high in my estimation. No one, but no one will ever dictate to me in such a highly personal matter as to my choice of my friends. It's true that I was born in a class of society and a neighborhood where recruits to communism could well be expected to originate, and who knows? If my life had continued in the conditions of poverty that I experienced then maybe I might have followed such a path myself. But as things turned out, I set out on a road that took me into a class of society no longer driven by need to resort to the fetters of soulless communism in order to seek improvement to an otherwise hopeless life.

"I have all I need and much more than I need and I would make a strange bedfellow in the Communist Party. If I had had any communist leanings I would certainly not, during the McCarthy period, have made what I thought was a comic remark, which in fact really began the hate campaign against me. That incident was so stupid as to be almost unbelievable. All that happened was this: I was invited to be a guest speaker at a huge rally called to launch a major appeal to encourage people to buy war bonds. When I walked on to the platform, I found a large number of high-ranking officers of the three services, while in the audience there was a great number of the well-heeled cream of American society. Quite off the cuff, I thought I would try and obtain a good laugh at the very start by putting everyone in a happy frame of mind before I opened my appeal. Looking around at the distinguished gathering I began by saying 'Hello comrades!' Instead of the roar of laughter that I expected, this comic and innocent utterance was received in almost total silence and my appeal, which followed, was scarcely treated with any greater enthusiasm. The following morning the papers declared that I had publicly confessed communist sympathies. I was thunderstruck, and wished that my participation in an appeal had been made in England to an English audience whose inborn sense of humor would undoubtedly have given my opening remarks the nuance that was intended.

"From then on I was forever being got at by people who seemed to be influenced by Senator McCarthy, that they had themselves succumbed to the same lunacy. I was even compelled on one occasion to temporarily cease shooting on one of my pictures in order to attend a special hearing where a group of men grilled me as if I were a murder suspect. When I was called upon to attend a second such charade, I refused to do so and this, plus other accumulative aggravations from all sides, made me make the irrevocable decision to leave the USA for good. So anxious was I to escape from this nightmare of injustice that Oona and I took only a few days to finalize our plans and to sail from New York, taking with us as much of our personal liquid assets as we could.

"No, Eric, I never have been and never will be a communist and if communism produces people just half as bad as those that so ill used me, it must be a very bad philosophy indeed."

Thanks to this conversation, plus the odd time or two the subject was touched upon again, plus the fact that during the twenty years that we worked together I got to know him very well indeed, I am absolutely convinced that he never was a communist, never even thought of becoming one, and never supported communism, either directly or indirectly. The fact that he was hounded out of the United States will remain a cruel and barbaric act unworthy of the honor of a great nation. It is true that the main harassment came from a comparatively small sector, i.e., McCarthy and his henchmen and the gutter press, but it seems a shame to me that the great majority of the American people did not rise up en masse in defense of him. In view of all he had done for America through the motion picture industry and for the very real pleasure that he gave to countless millions of Americans, it would have been a nice gesture if they had shown some loyalty to him when he had been attacked by a Gestapo-like clique that was not worthy enough even to tie his shoelaces.

I recall that one evening during dinner, at which the French ambassador was one of the guests, the ambassador asked Charlie how many staff he needed to run the Manoir. "Fifteen," was Charlie's reply, at which the Frenchman, with a look of incredulity, retorted, "Mon dieu, Charlie, that is more than we have at the embassy." Doubtless this large payroll contributed to the tremendous outlay needed to keep things going, a fact of life that seemed to cause him a great amount of worry. Back in 1958 he told me that his expenses were in excess of two hundred thousand dollars a year. He maintained that it was only by living in Switzerland that he could afford to carry this burden. He would have preferred to have lived and educate his children in England but just could not afford to do so. All of this was, of course, part of the same phobia about becoming poor again, and knowing how financially sound he really was, I never took his agonizing over money very seriously.

Whatever else can be said about Charlie, there is no doubt that he pulled himself up from the squalor and deprivation of his early life solely through his own efforts and determination. I once expressed to him my admiration for the fact that he was so well-spoken and in command of the English language, and yet had been brought up with practically no education whatsoever. He disclosed that from the moment he could think for himself at all, he was determined to get out of the strata of society in which he found himself, and when at the age of twelve he began to earn a meager sum working as a lather boy in a barber shop, he put aside a few pennies every week until he had sufficient money to purchase a dictionary. From then on he studied the book and tried to commit to memory the meaning and correct pronunciation of at least six words a day. He reckoned that by the time he was twenty-one years old he had acquired a vocabulary of some fifteen thousand words.

Perhaps it was because of this self-tuition that he was so extraordinarily pleased when Leeds University gave him an honorary doctorate of literature, which was followed by an honorary doctorate from Oxford in June 1962 and an honorary doctorate from Durham University in July 1962. Perhaps it's a good spot while considering the achievements of an uneducated boy, to record the fact that by the end of the 1950s, fifty-seven biographies had been written about Charlie and that number since then has doubled. All of them resided in his study and he had read every word of them. He also invited me to borrow any of them that I chose. I read quite a few of them and found the annotations written in the margins in Charlie's handwriting more interesting and amusing than the books themselves. The book that he preferred above all others, for reasons he never disclosed, was *The Art of Cine-Plastics,* by Elie Faure.

I have already mentioned the beautiful Steinway grand piano on which I worked. It was tuned regularly and kept at concert pitch. The instrument had been chosen for him by the famous Swiss concert pianist Clara Haskil, one of the world's greatest exponents of Beethoven. He would always ask the great musicians that he invited to visit from time to time to play. He was particularly pleased when Artur Rubenstein, who had been invited to supper one evening after giving a recital in Lausanne, offered to play and complimented him upon its perfection.

Charlie really loved that piano and he would spend many hours each week attempting to play it. I found it deeply distressing watching and listening to his efforts to do so. Even when he managed to get some sort of melody with his first three fingers of the right hand—the only ones he ever succeeded in using, in the key of F, his favorite key—the minute he started to try and use the left hand frequent discords resulted and he would curse vehemently in his frustration. Although it was his limited ability to play that resulted in my working with him, I did feel deeply sorry that he had not been able to find time to develop a talent that would have meant so much to him. Incidentally, every time Charlie stayed at the Savoy in London, a small grand piano was always moved into the drawing room of his suite.

Charlie had copies of all his movies specially printed in 16mm. They were stored in the basement in a room fitted with thermostatically controlled temperature in order to keep the films in mint condition. Occasionally after dinner, especially when guests were being entertained, Oona would suggest showing a film. This idea was always greeted with enthusiasm but when Oona would go on to suggest a particular film, Charlie would invariably protest and say, "I hate that one Mummy," or "Do I have to watch that again?" But once the film had commenced it was quite obvious that he was thoroughly enjoying it, whatever its title.

Charlie made it a rule that under no circumstances should we be interrupted while working, and even Oona would remain in an adjacent room, writing letters or working on petite pointe, of which she was very fond. Likewise the children were also barred, except for a moment or so before meals were announced and if they had been invited on their return from their various boarding schools.

I was therefore absolutely dumbfounded when Oona came in one day and told Charlie that a charming little Portuguese couple, devoted fans of his, would like to see him. He turned angrily to Oona and said, "Have you taken leave of your senses? You, above all people, know that we are not to be disturbed." She waited quietly for him to finish with what I would describe as a wry smile on her face and then, ignoring his outburst, said quietly, "Would it make any difference, dear, if I were to tell you that they have brought with them a dozen bottles of the finest port from their vineyards in Portugal, which they would like to present to you personally?"

There was utter silence for a second, then, giving a little cough Charlie said, "We mustn't be too hard. They have come a long way." Then in an aside to me he muttered, "One must make exceptions now and then, Eric." So saying he got to his feet with remarkable agility, and turning back to Oona said, "Come on, what are you waiting for, why don't you show them in?"

They were indeed a very charming couple and Charlie was sweet and agreeable to them, going out of his way to make sure they enjoyed their visit. They took up half an hour of our work time, but later when we both tried the port we wholeheartedly agreed that this was a small price to pay. This beautiful amber port was quite exquisite and emphasized just how poor are all the imitations. We drank it with cheese that very evening and many evenings thereafter. Charlie afterward instructed Oona to the effect that should, in the future, any Portuguese people be seen staggering toward the door carrying a crate of bottles, she must let them in immediately.

Talking of cheese, Stilton was his favorite, although good old-fashioned English cheddar ran a close second. I always brought a lump of it with me from England, together with four pairs of Scotch Kippers, which he absolutely adored, plus crumpets, pork sausages, and treacle tart. Two other fine edible items that both he and I enjoyed were a luxury cream cheese called Vecherin, and Creme de Bulle, a very thick cream, both entirely Swiss and produced locally thanks to the rich pastures on which the animals fed.

From my very first visit to Vevey I became aware of the tremendous authority Charlie exercised over his children. He could be very affectionate to them and he was in no way cruel or unreasonable, but he demanded and in the main received the respect he considered due to him. His extremely stern approach indeed guaranteed that they would make great efforts to avoid incurring his wrath.

I once asked Pinnie, one of the nannies, if Charlie ever resorted to corporal punishment. She just laughed and said, "He gives them the length of his tongue and that's enough."

He rarely watched television. He considered it a complete waste of time and although he possessed a set, it was very rarely switched on and then only to watch the world news. Whenever any of the children were at home they were obliged first of all to do their homework and then to do their practice on the upright piano kept on the top floor. He confided in me that he was determined that his children should not be denied the pleasures of playing the piano as he had been.

For my part, I think that children need discipline and that much of the present trouble with the youth of today stems from the lack of it. However, the Chaplin brood didn't see it that way and they resented his disciplined approach; almost every one of them could not wait to leave home just as soon they were old enough. Oddly enough, the fact that their parents were wealthy actually contributed toward their resentment and desire to go. They were cosseted and cushioned against all worries and responsibilities and lacked for nothing, and yet they were utterly bored most of the time with their lives at the Manoir.

Vicky tried to overcome the tedium of life at home by cultivating a number of pen pals and from this, several lasting friendships resulted. She had a lovely personality and a wonderful sense of humor and also a fine gift for mimicry. She was without doubt a special favorite of Charlie's. When she left the Manoir and went off to live in Paris with a French actor, Jean-Baptiste Thierrée, he really went to pieces. No doubt his pride was hurt, but as he said to me, "I loved her as I do all my other children and I gave her everything she wanted. Why should she repay me in this way?" I tried to reason with him and suggested that the fact that she had everything she wanted materially could have been the reason for her departure and a desire to see what life was like in the real world. After all, hadn't he always expressed pride and pleasure at having, by his own efforts, fought his way from poverty to a better life. He lifted his head from his hands and with watery eyes retorted angrily, "If she doesn't want my money you'd have thought she would have wanted my love." "I'm sure she does," I said. "The fact that she has decided to stand on her own two feet doesn't mean that she values your affection any the less. If you help her over this period now, her feelings for you will increase."

In response to this Charlie jumped to his feet and, literally quivering with rage, shouted, "Help her! Help her! She will never, and I mean never, set foot in this house again." At that I got up as well and putting my arm around his shoulders I said, very quietly, "Charlie, don't be silly. If Vicky's face should suddenly appear round that door you would throw your arms about her and say, 'Welcome home.' So don't talk such rot."

Without another word he walked out of the room and out of the house and I watched as he paced slowly round his favorite walking place. He had a battle to fight and he could only fight it on his own, so I left him there and carried on with my music revision. I subsequently learned that Jean-Baptiste Thierrée had success in such films as *Muriel* before marrying Vicky. His heart was set on a career as a clown, creating a circus with Vicky after they had married. Many years later I had the pleasure of seeing and enjoying "Le Cirque Imaginaire" (recently renamed Le Cercle Invisible) in London and meeting Vicky again, her husband, and two children—both of whom appeared in the show.

As the months went by Charlie began to accept the situation, even if not approving of it, and when Vicky finally married Jean-Baptiste she was able to come home and be received by Charlie with the warmth that I prophesied. She explained how hard their life was working a circus, the need for every person to share the heavy work, as well as putting their energies and talents into the show, sharing their meager profits and the terrible conditions in which they sometimes lived. This softened Charlie's heart and made him feel that however unsatisfactory the liaison, at least Vicky must really love her husband to be able to put up with it.

When in the fullness of time, a telegram arrived from their little flat in Paris announcing the birth of a daughter, Aurelia, the excitement engendered in the Manoir was something I shall never forget. Oona, together with Charlie's cousin, Betty Chaplin Tetrick, who was staying there, dashed into the town to purchase a layette and numerous other essentials and gifts appropriate to the arrival of a new baby. Charlie demanded that they should set out immediately after dinner and travel throughout the night to Paris. So it was that Oona and Betty, with Renato the chauffeur at the wheel and a car loaded with luggage, set off in the darkness for the long and tiring journey.

I must place on record that in the midst of all this excitement Oona found time to worry about our welfare over the couple of days they would be away. I remember she turned to us, I was well into my fifties and Charlie considerably more, and said, "Will you two boys please tell me what you would like Mary (the cook) to prepare for your meals while I am away?" I was pleased that she should be so thoughtful when she was so busy getting ready to go. Charlie, just as soon as she was out of his sight, became very irritable and edgy. He simply hated her being away from him, even though he had, on this occasion, insisted upon it himself. We had a most trying and difficult day together, the situation only relieved when a telegram was received from Oona saying that they had arrived safely. It seemed to act as a salve to his fiery temper and the remaining period of her absence became slightly more bearable.

This incident, depicting the pain that even a two-day parting gave to Charlie, typifies the deep and genuine feelings they had for one another. There have been many and varied snide remarks made about their marriage, due to the disparity in their ages, but in every case they have been made by people who have never had any personal contact whatsoever with either of them. It is true that he had been married before and it's equally true that these marriages were not successful. Why that was so and how the blame could be proportioned, is something on which I certainly cannot possibly express an opinion. Charlie was, as I well know from personal experiences, a difficult man to get on with and maybe his former wives could not adjust to that.

However, even though he was, without doubt, fond of the opposite sex that does not make him a lecherous individual or an evil one as his enemies would suggest. The failure of his marriages was probably due to the fact that his wives never turned out to be the soul mates he was so desperately seeking. In saying that I might give the impression that Charlie was the typical misunderstood husband, but it just wasn't like that. It was simply that in order to give expression to his tremendous artistic talents he really did need a wife who was something special, and Oona was just such a special person. That there was thirty-six years difference between them, he was fifty-four when they married and she was eighteen, proved to be no barrier to a successful marriage, as their thirty-two years of married life bears witness, and my own observation of that marriage, over twenty of those years, confirms it.

If there were anything scandalous or offbeat in their relationship and I was prepared to betray their trust and friendship, then the inclusion of it here would certainly help to sell many more books. The truth is, however, that there is absolutely no scandal to relate and the success of their marriage could be envied by many, many people. It was, in every sense of the word, a love match and one that was to last throughout the thirty-four years they spent together.

Their deep affection for each other was something that I always felt while in their presence. When their eyes met they would be full of mutual tenderness; she would frequently go over to him and kiss him affectionately on the forehead and he would respond with "Little Poopchik," a term of affection the origin of which remained beyond my understanding! I have even on a number of occasions been sitting next to Charlie at the piano when she has entered the salon, walked over to him, looked into his eyes, kissed him, and departed without a word. In view of the fact that this was done during the periods of "No disturbance under any circumstances," it emphasizes the depths of love and affection that could even enable her to risk his wrath by breaking the rules in expressing them. I cannot remember a single occasion when we were travelling together by car or train that they did not sit holding hands, and neither had eyes for anyone else. Indeed the only people who ever tried to date Oona were his two sons by his former marriage to Lita Grey, Sydney and Charlie Jr., who were always trying to take her out but inevitably received the "brush off," as she quite obviously had no interest for anyone other than their father.

On the first occasion that I met Oona's mother, Agnes Boulton, we were having dinner together in my apartment in London. She told me that her daughter had emphatically announced to her that as long as she lived she would never love any other man but Charlie. Her feelings certainly did not change throughout *his* lifetime.

CHAPTER 4

$\mathscr{A}$t one period of my life in the sixties, I took over the proprietorship of the Hotel Strand Continental in London. With the competent staff I was lucky to have, I was able to continue with my professional activities. It was while checking facts and figures with the receptionist one day that I suddenly saw a silver-haired man walking up the stairs and moments later I was greeting Charlie. It was such a surprise, as I had no idea that he was coming to England. We were very soon ensconced in my private penthouse apartment where he told me the visit had to be a flying one as he had to return to the Savoy Hotel, where he was to attend a special press reception with Sophia Loren and Marlon Brando, stars of his new film. The reception was due to start at midday, almost exactly the time he arrived in my hotel! He explained that the film he was setting up, *A Countess from Hong Kong,* was for him a very special venture and he had suddenly felt quite unable to attend the reception without personally satisfying himself that I would be willing and able to work with him on the music. Hence the sudden and hurried walk from the Savoy to see me at my hotel.

I of course assured him that there was no question of my letting him down, and I would come over just as soon as he was ready. His joy and relief was most flattering and heartwarming and Charlie seemed to forget that he was already thirty minutes late for his own press reception, because he began to delve into the ins and outs of the picture, particularly the difficulty he was experiencing with Sophia Loren and Marlon Brando. It seemed that there was no love lost between them and this lack of rapport, and the temperamental outbursts it engendered, made the shooting of certain scenes extremely "hazardous." He was obliged, he said, on several occasions to take them to the side of the set and read the riot act. This usually produced peace and harmony for a bit and so made it possible for the filming to continue.

For my part I felt quite pleased to find that such great stars could be subjected to Charlie's temper as well as lesser mortals like myself. He also went to great lengths to explain the kind of music that was required, and before long the couple of minutes that he could spare had turned into an hour, and he didn't leave until 1:00 p.m. I have often wondered what sort of reception he had at the reception!

Shortly after this unexpected meeting I was back in Vevey, where, incidentally, I was no longer staying at the Hotel du Lac to which I was accommodated at the very beginning of my association with Charlie, but now always enjoyed the luxury of the first class Trois Couronnes Hotel. I had a most beautifully appointed room, en suite, on the first floor with a balcony overlooking Lake Leman and the Dent-du-Midi. When I expressed to Charlie my gratitude for such comfortable quarters he again illustrated that money really did figure into his thinking, in spite of what he had said previously, by replying that he was glad I liked it because it was more expensive than the Savoy! He added, however, perhaps to make me feel better lest I felt ashamed for causing him to part with so much, that he considered it only right that I should have the very best accommodation that could be provided.

He immediately got down to the task in hand, and it was soon apparent that *A Countess from Hong Kong* required an enormous amount of music. Charlie was bubbling over with enthusiasm and full of ideas. One was that in deference to gypsy blood that he claimed ran through the veins of some of his ancestors, one piece of music should have a distinctly gypsy flavor. I was able to produce, with his guidance, an ambitious composition, very difficult to play, which he called "Gypsy Czardas." Out of all the music that was finally created for the film, the waltz titled "She Is a Countess from Hong Kong" was Charlie's favorite.

To his marked irritation I disagreed that it was the best song, and explained that my partner and future wife, Phyllis, felt quite confident that the song "This Is My Song" would be the hit. I will always be proud of this particular piece as Phyllis was convinced that it was an absolute winner and how right she was. It was Italian in style, complimenting Sophia Loren, and the end product as heard in the film was typically Neapolitan and played on mandolins and violins as a feature throughout the picture. Charlie had confided in me long ago that he was not very good at lyric writing and usually placed that chore elsewhere. However, in the case of "This Is My Song" he worked on the words himself and spent an enormous amount of time and effort before finally completing the lyrics. When the film was eventually released it received a very mixed reception from the press, but "This Is My Song" received almost universal praise, just as had been predicted.

When I returned to Switzerland to start work on *The Circus* he greeted me with, "Eric, I'm sure that you'll be delighted to know that we're off the hook." I asked him what that meant and he went on to explain that all the money that he had personally invested in the film had been retrieved. I congratulated him and said I was convinced that this situation had been brought about to a great extent by the song I had said would be a hit. To my surprise he admitted his error of judgement and gave Phyllis and me full credit for accurately forecasting the potential commercial success of that particular number, but his generosity stopped there!

Apart from the piano, which Charlie had tried so hard but so unsuccessfully to master, he had also earlier in his career undergone a great desire to play the violin. For some reason he felt he had greater dexterity in the fingers of the right hand and that he would thus have a better chance of succeeding if he used it instead of the left as all other violinists do. He decided to have a special violin made with the fingerboard reversed and for a while he achieved some limited amateur success. However, the instrument had serious limitations, and he soon discarded it and returned to the piano, the mastery of which was always to elude him.

My marriage unhappily ended after nearly thirty years. I had formed a partnership with professional singer Phyllis O'Reilly, and while working in Vevey on one occasion I arranged a cabaret date for her at one of the swanky hotels in Montreux. As soon as Oona heard about this she invited Phyllis up for afternoon tea. Needless to say she was thrilled to bits and I was very gratified at the way Charlie received her and made every effort to be an agreeable host. He even went so far as to break his own sacrosanct rules concerning the "No disturbance under any circumstances during working hours." I was obliged to continue working as normal while he went off with Phyllis and conducted her on the grand tour. It was indeed a great honor! While coming down the marble staircase Phyllis happened to notice what was, of course, a genuine

Constable. The minute her eyes lighted upon it she exclaimed, "My uncle has one exactly like that." Charlie threw back his head and laughed and then said, "Oh dear he must be a very rich man, I'd always thought that mine was the only one." Was her face red! After that amusing incident they got on splendidly and spent a long time on the patio discussing the merits of their respective children. On subsequent visits he always asked Phyllis to sing and on many occasions he would insist on her including "This Is My Song," as he said no other artist could sing it as well as she did.

One outstanding event at the Manoir, which I recall with great pleasure, was the occasion of Josie's wedding to a charming Greek business man, Nicky Sistovaris. In June 1969, I flew over especially for the occasion. On arrival at the Manoir, I joined the long queue of guests waiting to be formally received by the Chaplins and the bride and bridegroom. They stood at the wide doors of the salon, which marked the entrance to a flower festooned corridor through which one passed in order to enter the enormous marquee that had been erected on the grounds. As soon as I neared the head of the queue and Charlie saw me, he immediately left Oona's side and almost ran across the room and without even a formal word of greeting, said, "Eric, I have a most marvelous idea for the theme music of our next film, *The Freak*," and he at once began to go into rapturous details.

This was too much for me and I said, "Stop Charlie, for goodness sake! Of course the music is important to you but this is your daughter's wedding day! It's her day, a day for eating, drinking, and celebration, not for talking about music, and films. For once, this must take second please."

He looked quite vexed and remonstrated, but reluctantly agreed to postpone his enthusiasm until after lunch the following day. The party really went with a swing. Two bands were in attendance to ensure that there would be a continuous sound of music, and the champagne flowed like water.

The guest list read like a great chunk of the theatrical "Who's Who," and I had the pleasure of meeting many famous people, including the "Master" himself, Noel Coward. As usual he was surrounded by his court of ardent admirers, and when I was introduced he just gazed at me in silence for some moments before speaking. I have subsequently come to the conclusion that this hesitation was a long practiced device to gain time in which to ponder on every utterance before it issued forth from his lips, lest it might lack the Coward nuances he knew were expected, indeed demanded, by a worshiping world. At last, removing his cigarette holder from his mouth, he said "So, dear boy, you are the magnificent manipulator who has to grapple with the task of setting the great man's musical musings onto paper." I made to reply but a quick flick of his cigarette holder clearly indicated that the Master had not finished speaking. "It must be a terribly, terribly tough assignment." Feeling that his now motionless cigarette holder indicated permission to speak, I smiled and said, "Oh, I don't know. The scars have all healed and a bittersweet association is better than none at all." Noel laughed, the courtiers laughed, I laughed, and it was all over. I had been received by the Master, whose restive mind was already directed toward other guests and further outlets for his incomparable repartée.

I got back to the hotel in the early hours of the morning, snatched a few hours sleep and then returned to the Manoir, where I found Charlie ruefully surveying a mountain of empty champagne bottles near the huge marquee in which the celebrations had taken place. "This wedding must have cost you a fortune," I said. He slowly turned his head and retorted with a voice, in which I thought I detected a note of mock bitterness, "This wedding has cost me so much that I'm going to give my next daughter and her husband-to-be a lump sum of money to elope—it'll be cheaper!"

After that cryptic comment we made our way to the salon where I quickly transcribed to manuscript the idea for the melody to which he had referred on the previous day. I put in quite a lot of effort on the piece and was pleased with the result, but for purely mechanical reasons it was never used for the film *The Freak*, in which Vicky was to star, but it did become the theme music for *The Kid.*

I returned to London later that day after finding, with pleasure, that my account at the Trois Couronnes Hotel had been settled by Oona, a gesture I greatly appreciated.

When I next went over to work on another film, I found Charlie in a very good humor. He had just heard from Rachel Ford that she had finalized a deal with the mighty Mo Rothman, a former vice president of Columbia Pictures. It involved the distribution of the films Charlie still owned. The distribution deal made millions for Charlie.

All of this of course made a mockery of his declared anguish over the cost of Josie's wedding. I would have been less than human had I not compared his windfall of millions for which he had to do no real extra work whatever, with the modest remuneration I received for working flat out in helping to bring that windfall about. One would have thought that he would have found joy in spreading a little "largesse" around, if only to mark such staggering addition to his fortune, which would have been more than adequate for any age, let alone his. The truth is I don't think he ever considered for a moment that money could be as important to other people as himself. However, it occurred to me that this unexpected and enormous addition to his wealth would result in us, particularly myself, being able to take things easier, instead of working nonstop on the music, as if the money that would follow the completion of the film was absolutely essential to stave off starvation!

On hearing the news I said, "Well Charlie, we've worked hard and I'm sure you must be as tired as I am, so I expect you'll want to take things easy from now on." His reply simply staggered me. "I am far too busy to take things easy Eric, I've far too many things to do. I want to write another book and I intend to make a picture starring Geraldine and Vicky, and if you live long enough I hope you'll help me write an opera."

I asked him if he'd thought of the subject and Charlie replied that it would be based on the novel by Thomas Hardy, *Tess of the d'Urbervilles,* "ideally suitable for an opera."

He then went on to show me how the book would be split up into acts and scenes, which proved that he really had been thinking of it for some time. He saw the apprehension in my face as I contemplated with a musician's mind what a mammoth undertaking it would be, and he simply slapped me on the shoulder and said, "You're equal to it Eric. I know you are and what is more, we already have a venue for it when it's finished. The directors of the La Scala Opera House, Milan, have already told me that they would deem it a privilege if the La Scala were to be the first opera house in the world to present it." Upon reflection I realized that this interest in opera must have come about because of the performance of *Carmen* at La Scala, when the Chaplins were the special guests of the directors. At the end of the performance Maria Callas and all the other artists were brought to the Chaplins' box and presented to them. He afterward told me that that was when he had been urged to write an opera.

Some weeks earlier I had touched on the fact that Charlie would not allow his children to watch television because it was nonproductive, but as time passed his attitude, at least with regard to himself, changed completely, and he had a large color television set installed in his study.

Here, at the end of the day, he would often spend a lot of time watching various programs but he had a preference for films. These he watched, not just as a member of the audience but as a critic. Throughout the film he would say such things as, "What a ridiculous angle for that shot! Why didn't they do this or why didn't they do that?" When he wasn't making comments on the production itself he would make forthright criticisms of the actors' performances. I never once observed him watching a film in silence.

When I first joined up with Charlie, he was still extremely active and he frequently played tennis before breakfast. Having been coached by Bill Tilden while in Hollywood, he could play a respectable game. Oona quite often would take him on. He also made use of the well-heated swimming pool, but only occasionally. As he got older he began to take even shorter walks in the garden. He tried to justify this by saying that he felt unsteady on his feet, so I suggested that he use a walking stick. His reaction was decidedly militant and he said, "Damn it, Eric, my pride won't let me use a walking stick!" I quickly retorted, "Blast your pride! Better to swallow your pride than break an arm or leg, and apart from that a stick has been the life long symbol of Charlie the Tramp, so it won't be a new thing for you to carry a stick."

He went off muttering, but a few days later, without any further comment, he started to use one. I also observed to him on one occasion that entertaining guests at the Manoir was considerably less than it used to be and he explained, quite seriously to me, "If we accept an invitation to dinner it will only mean that we have to invite them back, so we save ourselves a lot of bother by declining."

When the much-deserved but long-delayed knighthood was conferred on Charlie in March 1975, he went to England to receive the honor from the queen. Afterward he held a celebration party at the Savoy. It was a most enjoyable occasion. Phyllis and I were included among the guests. While we were there by invitation, two people, Sir Harold Wilson and Lady Falkender, just turned up unexpectedly. It so happened that Charlie, for some reason, admired Harold Wilson greatly and was very pleased when he appeared, and he insisted on a photograph being taken of them together. When he returned home, an enlargement of this picture was hung in the corridor leading to his suite so that he might see it every time he passed by. When he began to have difficulty with walking and was obliged to use the downstairs cloakroom quite often during the day, Oona explained that she had had it transferred there because he would then be able to look at the picture as often as he wanted. However, I have no doubt that many will feel that it was a perfect location.

I cannot leave the downstairs cloakroom without referring to a most amusing incident that occurred one Christmas. It had been the custom, just prior to Christmas Day, for members of a local choir to trudge up the steep hill from Vevey and position themselves by the main door of the Manoir to give a performance of carols. On this occasion Charlie had an urgent need to use the lavatory, where he sat on "the throne" but unfortunately had forgotten to pull over the curtains.

Happily engaged with the business in hand and in deep contemplation, he failed to notice the arrival of the choir until they burst into song just a few feet from the window. He was absolutely taken aback because although while sitting they could only see his head and shoulders, if he were to stand up the "herald angels" would take off in alarm! The choir was obviously quite impressed by the sight of him in the window because they mistakenly thought that he was so eager to hear them sing that he had stationed himself at this vantage point well in advance of their arrival. As it was, he had to sit there with his trousers down for half an hour, beaming at them every now and then and clapping animatedly after each carol.

It wasn't until the last of them had passed into the house that he was able to get up, pull the curtains and adjust himself before joining them. The leader of the group expressed their great satisfaction at having found Mr. Chaplin so impatiently awaiting their performance! Charlie's reply could not have been bettered. He thanked them and said that their singing had literally rooted him to the spot!

Incidentally, Charlie hated Christmas. He would put on a show for the sake of his family, but he was always glad when it was over. His excuse was that Christmas reminded him of his workhouse days and general poverty. I feel, however, that the truth probably is that like a well-known Dickensian character he regarded Christmas as an expensive annual event that he would rather do without!

People have frequently asked me if we laughed a lot together and I have to answer immediately that Charlie, like many other comics that I have known, was in essence a somewhat gloomy personality. He was only truly happy when we were working, although I must confess that during off-duty periods I would sometime tell him the odd joke or two that I had heard prior to flying over to Switzerland to work with him. One story that he particularly enjoyed hearing was the classic about the man who was in a small village in the outskirts of Yorkshire and was knocking at the doors of these remote cottages, carrying a collecting box in his hands. He noticed a particular attractive cottage with the front door festooned with clematis. Without hesitation, he opened the garden gate and boldly knocked at the front door, which was eventually answered by a very elderly lady wearing a lace doily on her head. On asking what he wanted, the man replied, "Madam, I am collecting on behalf of the Accrington Stanley Boys Brass Band," to which the old lady answered, "I am sorry, you must forgive me, I am extremely deaf and cannot hear a word you are saying." Not to be outdone, the man once again repeated his request that he was collecting on behalf of the Accrington Stanley Boys Brass Band and the old lady replied, "You are wasting your time young man, I cannot hear a word you're saying," at which the man turned on his heel and retreated toward the garden gate. As he reached it the old lady shouted out, "Shut the gate," and the young man shouted back, "Fuck the gate." The old lady shouted out just as vehemently, "And fuck the Accrington Stanley Boys Brass Band." When I told the story to Charlie I did so in character—the old lady's quivering voice was not difficult to do and seemed to add credibility to the story. Oona came in the salon on hearing Charlie laughing so heartily and insisted that I tell her the story. I replied that I felt somewhat hesitant because it necessitated the use of a word that is not normally used in the best circles and in particular to a lady such as Oona. Her reaction was immediate and she told me in no uncertain terms that no bad words would ever shock her and that she knew them all, and so, somewhat reluctantly I repeated the anecdote, which once again received spontaneous laughter from her.

To complete these reminiscences of the "Boys Brass Band" story, I must hasten to add that James Mason, who I had previously met on several occasions and more recently at Josie's wedding reception, was currently staying at the Trois Couronnes in Vevey prior to travelling to Vienna to commence work as the star in a film that I think was titled *Emperor Josef.* When we bumped into each other at the hotel, he invited me to have lunch with him, and as it was my "day off"–Sunday—I readily accepted. During the course of the meal I thought that perhaps he might enjoy the joke that I had previously told Oona and Charlie. He, too, proved to be a most receptive audience and laughed heartily when I had finished telling it. After a most pleasant lunch we said our farewells and I added my good wishes for his personal success in the film that he was about to make.

The following morning, I was about to leave the hotel for a brief walk prior to being collected by the chauffeur, who would be taking me up to the Manoir to commence work with Charlie, when I noticed that James Mason was engaged in deep conversation with a group of important film executives at one of the carriage entrances of the cobblestone forecourt of this nineteenth-century hotel. On seeing this cluster of VIPs surrounding Mason, I decided that in order to prevent an intrusion on my part, it would be wiser for me to use the other carriage exit and had almost reached it, when I became aware that someone was running, quite noisily, on the cobblestone forecourt toward me. To my surprise it was James Mason, who breathlessly asked me if I would once again repeat the "tag" line of the joke that I had told him at lunch on the previous day. It only goes to show that we are all quite human, no matter how famous!

The hardest work for all concerned was when the moment came for carrying out the music balance at the recording studios. This task was made no easier because Charlie insisted on sitting in the control room with the engineers and myself and virtually directing the sensitivity of the various mikes in use. He would demand that this mike or that should predominate on this or that passage, and in general he tried to carry out the whole technical process, which the engineer and I could have managed quite satisfactorily on our own. Charlie would justify himself by saying that he was a perfectionist, implying that the balance engineer and particularly myself were not. I found these sessions so irritating that I would remain silent and let him chatter on, knowing that in the end we would have to try to do what was unquestionably correct. It was a most exacting science and just had to be done correctly. The sound had to have exactly the same level of volume throughout as far as possible. This was necessary because the music was continuous and as a result, the change over from reel to reel frequently involved the same piece of music, hence the necessity of matching the sound levels exactly.

Another highly technical process was known as "laying the track" and this involved painstaking work, lining up the recorded music, a most laborious business. Each and every prearranged cue for the various pieces of music had to be lined up with the actual frame of the appropriate piece of film. After the whole session had been completed to Charlie's satisfaction, there would follow a nail-biting period while the complete film was run through, reel by reel. With bated breath we would await Charlie's acceptance or otherwise of the "married" print and finished article.

As he began to get older it became apparent that he was beginning to lose his confidence because he would, just now and then, take the unprecedented step of asking my advice on some of the problems that would arise. If only he had been prepared to take a back seat all the time and allow the technicians and myself to do the job, which we were after all being paid to do, the embarrassing situation over *The Kid* would not have happened.

When the reels were run through and he confirmed his approval, I was anything but happy and knew that all was not well. However, as he had stamped his seal of approval on it, I was in no position to voice my criticism. It was shortly after the music for this particular film was completed that Mo Rothman finalized a deal in which this film, plus another, *The Idle Class*, was to have its special premiere in New York, just prior to Charlie's trip to Hollywood in April 1972.

He was making the visit in order to receive the Honorary Academy Award from Daniel Tarradash, president of the Academy of Motion Picture Arts and Sciences. A private run through of *The Kid* was set up, at which, thankfully, Charlie was not present. As a result, there was strong criticism from all sides in regard to the music balance and it was realized that the film could not be presented to the public without damaging Charlie's reputation. This was a particularly important factor because the film was to be shown coast to coast, and would be seen by a great number of people who had never seen it before. A conference was called, the outcome of which was an unanimous agreement that under no circumstances whatsoever could Charlie be made aware that his work on the balancing was unacceptable; nevertheless, complete rebalancing had to be carried out. I was called upon by Mo Rothman to undertake this task and I was sworn to absolute secrecy. I honored that pledge throughout his life, and in fact am revealing it now for the very first time. I carried out the work at the International Post Film Production Studios on Greek Street, in London's West End, a very efficient organization run by Roger Cheryll. I used to almost break out in a cold sweat when I thought of the consequences should Charlie ever find out. The shock would have been frightening and could well have destroyed him. To him, his personal satisfaction was everything and no one but no one could ever make decisions concerning his films but him!

While on the subject of *The Kid* I must refer to a previous private showing of it, during which an extremely amusing incident occurred. In the latter part of the film there is a hilarious dream sequence and it was during this that Charlie suddenly turned to me and whispered, "Do you see that girl there? The one with the angels wings? Well, she is the mother of Charlie and Sydney." Without thinking I immediately asked, "What's her name?" There was a long silence during which Charlie stared at me blankly, as if I had asked the "64 Thousand Dollar Question" instead of just the name of his former wife. Then, snapping his fingers and gripping my arm tightly, he replied, "Oh, dear, this is terrible Eric. Do you know, I just can't remember!" I found myself thinking that Lita Grey would have felt flattered!

I sometimes think that although the secret about *The Kid* was kept from him, he was perhaps, deep in his subconscious mind, beginning to doubt his own ability to work on the music, because he began to delegate more and more of the work at the studios to me. I completed the balancing on *Pay Day*, *A Day's Pleasure*, *Sunnyside*, and *A Woman of Paris*, and during the whole time taken for this he seldom turned up at the studios at all. Happily for me he always seemed satisfied with my work and was generous with his compliments, but nothing else.

The gradual deterioration in Charlie's health was very distressing, especially when one remembered what an active man, both mentally and physically, he had been throughout his life. I remember one example of his deterioration, which happened when he and I were having our usual aperitif before dinner. Gino, the butler, entered the salon and announced that dinner was served, but Charlie made no signs of movement. After a few minutes I began to get up and Charlie, observing this, said, "Has he called us yet?"

His deteriorating condition brought increasing problems for Oona, for he could not bear her to be out of his sight. He was then, as always, a very demanding person and she became at times completely exhausted, especially during frequent bouts of illness, when she nursed him both night and day. She never knew what it was to have an unbroken night's rest, and yet she never grumbled or displayed any impatience.

I used to marvel at her attentiveness and her love and tenderness, which was as deep as at any time during their long marriage. When I told her how I admired her she merely said, "Charlie looked after me when I was young and needed looking after. It is now my turn to look after him. If love means anything at all, it must prevail in the bad times as well as the good."

However, it was obvious that this state of affairs could not continue and I urged her, in spite of Charlie's adamant declaration never to have a nurse, to employ one before she herself cracked up. So finally a very sweet and agreeable girl from South Africa was engaged and Charlie would suffer her to sit with him for certain periods during the day and so enable Oona to get some rest, do some local shopping, and deal with the day-to-day running of the Manoir.

As the years went by, Charlie found it more and more difficult to think of ideas for the music and he would leave a great deal of it to me. I would suggest what I thought he would like, and then play it over to him for his approval, which was usually forthcoming. When I arrived to work with Charlie on *A Woman of Paris*, the last film on which I worked with him, he looked quite weak and ill. His very first words to me were "Eric, I haven't got an idea in my head for the music of this film."

I was very distressed to find him in such a state and I could see that he found even talking quite an effort. I therefore told him not to worry but that when I had finished each piece and played it over to him, he need only nod or shake his head to indicate his judgment of it. Thus it was that the very last music that I was to work on at the Manoir was completed in a few weeks and accepted by the employer and friend who, when I left the Manoir, I thought I was destined never to see again.

Shortly after returning to England I wrote to Rachel Ford in Paris, where she was in sole charge of all Chaplin business and personal affairs. This is an extract from my letter to her written on October 28, 1976.

I also think that you will agree that in the past year or so, Charlie's ability to communicate has regrettably deteriorated tremendously. This particularly applies where music is concerned and you must believe me when I tell you that when I arrived at Vevey last year to commence work on "A.W.O.P.," his first words to me were "Eric, I haven't an idea in my head" to which I jokingly replied, "Never mind, I'll play some ideas to you and you can throw them out or accept them as you see fit." Knowing his style of composition as intimately as I do after so many years, I was able to suggest melodies and ideas that were agreeable to him. As a result I can truthfully say that the majority of the music stemmed from my brain. It also enabled the music for the film to be completed in Switzerland in three weeks instead of three months which might easily have been the time taken if Charlie had had to compose every bar of music required for a film lasting more than one hour twenty mins.

I never received a reply to this letter and was disappointed to find that no additional screen credit was given when *A Woman of Paris* was shown. I was equally disappointed that no ex gratia payment was forthcoming in appreciation of the efforts I had made.

Early in 1977, I was invited to go to Switzerland to compile an anthology of Charlie's best music from all of his movies to which a music track had been added. It was a monumental task and entailed my listening to scores of tapes in order to choose which music would be commercially viable and attractive to listen to. Charlie placed his personal study at my disposal and the whole place was quickly transformed into a miniature recording studio. I was given a free hand to record a compilation of music that could be issued as a record album.

On one occasion there was a tap at the door of Charlie's study, and when Oona entered, she told me that Charlie was sitting in his wheelchair in the corridor outside and wondered if I would object to his coming in. He promised that he would not interfere with my choice of music for the album that I was endeavoring to compile.

All was going well until I accidentally dropped the feather-light arm of his record player and the needle slithered across the record and made the inevitable sound of scratching the surface. Suddenly, Charlie, who hadn't spoken a word for about two days, yelled out, "Eric, don't fuck it about." Oona and I collapsed with laughter for here was the Charlie we knew so well, reprimanding me and becoming for a few moments his normal self. Regrettably, this sudden return to vocal normality was only temporary and he immediately became uncommunicative for the remainder of the time that I spent at the Manoir completing the album. As it turned out, all my time and efforts proved to be a waste of time because Andre Kostelantz had only just completed an album of Charlie's best compositions, which was currently on sale in the record shops and stores in the United States and Europe. It was wisely decided that this would not be the appropriate time to issue a similar collection and the idea was postponed indefinitely.

I have been relating the story of my twenty years' association with Chaplin and indeed much of my time was spent in this capacity. However, my remuneration from that source was not large enough to enable me to meet my financial obligations and there was no retainer, so I had to seek engagements elsewhere when not actually working with or for him.

However, on reflection I must add that one of my most treasured possessions is a book he gave me entitled *My Life in Pictures*, in which he had written "To Eric, with my love and respect. Charlie."

One of the penalties for making oneself readily available is that a booking can fall on Christmas Day and such was the case in 1977. Phyllis and I were due to appear at the Prince's Hotel, and several others in Eastbourne, and we were trying to catch up on our sleep before going there. We had not reached our bed until 1:00 a.m. and it therefore came as a bit of a blow when the phone rang at 5:00 a.m. and I had to struggle to get my thoughts together before answering it. I was, however, jerked into complete consciousness when the voice on the phone told me that Charlie had died at 4:00 a.m. My loudly expressed and shocked reply aroused Phyllis more than the phone had done, and she sat up, wide awake, as I replaced the receiver and told her that Charlie had passed on.

We sat in silence, trying to grasp the fact that the world was now a place in which one of the greatest personalities of our time no longer played a part. The news was not unexpected because his rapid deterioration in health had been all too evident over the past couple of years, but when it actually came, it was still a shock. As Charlie's great personality and drive had slowly disappeared, I found my visits to Vevey more and more distressing. I had to be a nurse as well as a musical associate. He needed physical help all the time and I was glad to be able to serve him in this way. When our musical cooperation finally reached a point where he could only nod his head to signify his approval of the music I had produced in the vein I hoped he would favor, I realized that he had lost the ability to fight and would inevitably slip away from us before very long.

We finally got up, dressed and sat over a cup of tea and talked together of the Charlie Chaplin that we both knew. God knows he had his faults and I have not attempted to hide them in this book. He was tightfisted, he was arrogant, and he could be extremely bad tempered and difficult to work with, and no doubt he had many other of the imperfections that could be attributed to most people. But in spite of all this, we loved him and were proud to call him a friend, and we knew we would miss him terribly.

Because we knew the truth of the love that Oona had for him, we were well aware how sad and distressed she would be, so I sent a telegram to her before setting off for our engagements in Eastbourne. When the moment came for us to begin our performance I decided to say a few words to the audience. I told them that I knew they would understand just how difficult the performance would be for us that evening, but that Charlie would be the first to say "the show must go on." Perhaps, however, they would forgive us if we changed our intended program and substituted the music and songs associated with Charlie Chaplin. At the end of our act the audience gave a standing ovation, and it was obvious that they were trying to reach out to Charlie through us, as if they felt a desperate need to demonstrate their gratitude in our presence for all the joy he had given them. It was very moving and we were glad to seek the refuge of our dressing room.

We packed in silence, loaded the car, and then set off along the road to drive to our home in Barnes. We passed many gaily lit Christmas trees and we could see and even, on occasion, hear the sounds of jollification as the people celebrated this festive period. For us, however, our thoughts were dominated by the sad news. And no matter how we tried to catch the spirit of Christmas and converse about other matters, inevitably Charlie's name would spring back to the lips of one of us as we remembered this or that. I managed to lighten our spirits when I said, "Well at least he won't be worrying about the cost of Christmas this year!" We both laughed and then I felt decidedly guilty at having made the joke and said, "Sorry, Charlie!"

Phyllis, in her usual practical way, said, "Why say sorry? Surely Charlie, above all, would wish people to laugh, and if he knew, would probably laugh at what you've just said, so let's get things in proportion." She smiled gently and continued, "He had a long life, he achieved a great deal and he passed away peacefully. We are sad that he has gone, but he would not wish us to turn this into a Greek tragedy."

I knew that she was right and said so. "One struggles to achieve something; some reach a pinnacle like Charlie and then its all over and often forgotten, but not so with him. So now, let's snap out of it and get down to deciding what we are going to do for the shows on the twenty-sixth and on the following day as well as the big one on New Year's Eve."

So we started to exchange ideas as we drove on through the night just as we had done on many, many nights. There would be much more driving in the dark ahead of us as we pursued our hectic lives. Run-of-the mill engagements as well as television and radio ones would be taken up with equal enthusiasm. We would still be doing what we had done all our lives, a job of our own choice, and not everyone is lucky enough to do that. The houses gave way to open fields and we felt the familiar feeling of being out in limbo as it were, neither at home, or entertaining. This gray vale through which we sometimes passed in the quiet hours of the night always left us vulnerable to unhappy and nonproductive thoughts and never more so than on this occasion. We talked animatedly and finalized our program content for many shows to come but we were relieved when our headlights finally lit up the familiar buildings that heralded the approach to our own home.

I slumped into a chair and said, "So much for Christmas. The spirit never caught up with us did it?" Phyllis picked a bottle of my favorite brandy and poured some into a glass for me. She got her own favorite fruit juice and said, "Let's drink a toast to another spirit, that of Charlie who may even now be causing consternation among the angels as he floats above with a halo, which he has knocked into the shape of a bowler!" We raised our glasses, and I said, "For all the pleasure you have given through your films, 'crick in the neck' or not, thank *you* Charlie." We downed our drinks and then made our weary way to bed where we surrendered to the tender arms of Morpheus.

Index

Index

About the Author

*M*any books have been written about Charles Chaplin. Most of them are the result of research and material gathered from various sources and archives.

Eric James had had the privilege of knowing Charlie Chaplin personally for more than twenty years. Eric worked with him in the capacity of Music Associate, and during his frequent visits to Switzerland lived "en famille" at the Manoir de Ban in Vevey with Oona and Charlie.

The author is a musician of eminence and considerable experience. Chaplin was quick to recognize his talents at their first meeting at Shepperton Studios in 1956 where Eric was engaged to play piano for a short sequence of *A King in New York*, a film which Chaplin was directing. His expertise in fulfilling this specialized assignment was the primary reason for his being invited to assist Chaplin with the composition and arrangement of music for a large number of his films. After Eric had completed a seven week stint in Switzerland, the first of many similar assignments with Chaplin, he was told, "Eric you have done a good job... write your own screen credit." That was praise indeed and Eric modestly suggested "**ERIC JAMES**–Music Associate." Charlie readily agreed and it was in this capacity Eric remained until Chaplin's death in 1977.

This book is more than a musical profile of Charlie Chaplin. For not only does it reveal the writer's firsthand experiences with Charlie, but it also gives a true insight into Chaplin as he was in the relaxed atmosphere of his home. This intimate professional and personal relationship has enabled the author to give accurate answers to many questions that have been asked about Chaplin: What was he like to work with? Was he a genius? Was he a communist? Was his marriage to Oona a happy and successful one? Was he a generous man?

Many other questions are answered in this book. Originally it was hinted that it should be solely about Charlie Chaplin, but as Eric James himself has had a most colorful and interesting career, it was suggested that he write an autobiography instead. Shortly before Chaplin died, he presented Eric with a copy of his latest literary offering titled *My Life in Pictures*. On the flyleaf he wrote: "To Eric with my love and respect." Could any author ask for a finer dedication?